Comparative Religion in Education

Comparative Religion in Education

A Collection of Studies

Edited by

John R. Hinnells

Lecturer in Religious Studies
University of Newcastle upon Tyne

ORIEL PRESS

First published 1970

SBN (70 UK) 85362 074 1

Library of Congress Catalog Card No. 73-99784

Note

This book is based upon the Shap Conference held at Easter 1969 under the auspices of the Department of Adult Education of the University of Newcastle upon Tyne.

Published by
Oriel Press Limited,
27 Ridley Place,
Newcastle upon Tyne, NE1 8LH,
England.

Printed by
Northumberland Press Limited
Gateshead

Contents

The Editor gratefully inscribes the book
to the memory of
The late Rev. Dr Alasdair M. McKenzie
a great source of inspiration and a
devoted worker for religious studies

Foreword

by The Right Honourable EDWARD SHORT, M.P.,
Secretary of State for Education and Science

In this exciting decade new and challenging situations constantly confront us. We walk along Piccadilly or Oxford Street and hear snatches of conversation in many different languages; we turn the knob of our radio sets and the ether is a babel of tongues; we enter schools in many of our cities and are surrounded by children of a dozen races, cultures and creeds. In the learning situations which our schools have to provide it is important that this diversity should not prove a barrier, but an enrichment. It can surely be so if we equip ourselves with the knowledge which dispels ignorance and the conviction that builds friendship and understanding.

In this connection Mr Hinnells' book will, I believe, be widely welcomed. The problems which confront the teacher are, in the first place, to inform himself adequately of the tenets and character of the different faiths and philosophies which now have their adherents in our classrooms, and staffrooms, and secondly to relate them to each other so that they complement rather than conflict. He will find this book, in which each chapter is from the pen of an acknowledged authority in the field of which he writes, a most valuable guide. It is concerned with more than a simple examination of different religions and beliefs. The history, the purpose and the scope of comparative religion are considered in turn, the different ethical approaches are analysed, and resultant teaching problems are frankly and constructively faced. It should be of service not only to teachers, but to all concerned for the religious and philosophical education of the young.

Editor's Introduction

From a number of different quarters the suggestion is being made that the comparative study of religion, or teaching of World Religions, should play a greater part in the educational system than it does at present. The subject is to some extent being thrust before the public through mass media coverage of other nations, greater travel, and the presence of immigrant communities in Britain. The Humanist supports a wider study of religion to overcome what he considers to be the 'parochial outlook' of traditional RE; many people in education believe that it is important to cover religions other than Christianity or Judaism in order to give a wider and deeper understanding of religion, to stimulate thought, and to provide a more sensitive awareness of man; others believe that by understanding the culture and faiths of immigrants one of our greatest social problems can be alleviated. For these and other reasons, many universities, colleges and schools have begun or expanded their teaching of comparative religion. Admirable though this may be it is important that the enormous problems involved are not ignored or taken too lightly.

This book, in bringing together the views of a number of specialists, examines carefully the nature and scope of the subject at all levels of education. Scholars have been far from unanimous in their appraisal of the discipline. To some, as Dr Sharpe shows, the subject has been the key to explain away Christianity, to others it has been anathema. Even where the subject has been favoured there has been little agreement over the method by which it should be studied, indeed, even over the name to be given to it! The structure of the comparative study of religion, the variety of possible approaches, and the rather bewildering number of disciplines it spans philosophy, psychology, sociology, to say nothing of the languages, histories and cultures of the different religions) are discussed by Professor Smart. Teachers in colleges and schools are understandably cautious about the possibility of incorporating such disciplines into their syllabus. Yet the fruits to be gathered are such that they (see the surveys of Hinnells and Sharpe), together with Humanists (see Blackham's article), and Evangelical Christians (see Johnston's article), believe that an effort must be made. Perhaps one of the exciting possibilities of comparative religion is that it is a form of religious education where teachers of any religious faith, or those of none at all, can work together in all conscience and agreement. It is the practical aspect of the subject which appeals to so many. From an understanding of the beliefs of immigrants can grow a more sympathetic attitude to them as people, as Dr Parrinder's article shows. For all these reasons then it is important to look at the problems and methods of teaching comparative religion in schools (see Professor Hilliard's article).

Although progress must not be so slow that the whole process grinds to a halt, as all contributors stress, any advance must be made wisely, cautiously and patiently. By bringing together such different outlooks and by attempting to hear all sides it is hoped that this book makes a useful contribution to that advance.

JOHN R. HINNELLS

The Comparative Study of Religion in Historical Perspective

Eric J. Sharpe

It is scarcely necessary at the present time to draw attention to the remarkable popularity of 'world religions' as a subject for academic and semi-academic study in Western educational institutions. Universities, colleges of education, seminaries and theological colleges, secondary schools and part-time classes are all, in their various ways, attempting to meet what is in process of becoming a widespread popular desire for insights into the beliefs and practices of religions other than Christianity. The cause of this upsurge of enthusiasm for a subject which until only a few years ago remained the province of a very few specialists would provide a fascinating study in itself. Briefly (for this is not a subject we can undertake to examine in detail here) it seems that improved travel and communications, insistent questioning of the role of the West vis-à-vis non-Western nations and peoples, increased availability of information on the popular level, and the presence in the midst of Western societies of ever larger numbers of adherents of non-Western religious traditions, have combined with a growing feeling of disillusionment with organized Christianity and with the intellectual foundations of Western society to turn increasing numbers of people—and not least young people—towards a new quest for 'light from the East'. This phenomenon, particularly in its more extreme aspects, may be ephemeral. But for the present it is a fact of experience, which the educationalist would be unwise to attempt to ignore. And in view of the current crisis in religious education, it is imperative that we should know what may be involved in this new and apparently exotic orientation. Equally, we must know what is not involved, since newness and the quality of the exotic are poor recommendations for an academic subject.

It is, however, undeniable (however unfortunate it may be) that the words 'comparative religion' have long suggested something unorthodox and off-beat, and therefore, perhaps, a possible alternative to orthodoxy in a period when all orthodoxies are suspect. There are good historical reasons for this. But there are much better reasons for looking upon the comparative study of religion (CSR) as both a highly individual and a highly necessary field of study, related only incidentally to current emphasis in popular religious culture.

CSR is neither a very new nor a very old subject.[1] If two of its constituent elements are a degree of detachment from one's own religious tradition (i.e. the tradition of the society in which one happens to be placed) and a degree of interest in religious traditions other than one's own, then a good case might be made out for the subject having its origins in classical antiquity. But an academic subject, if it is to be studied at all consistently, must have an adequate method, and until the third quarter of the nineteenth century, this was precisely what it lacked. There had of course been earlier studies of certain world religions; but the motives from which these studies were undertaken varied greatly. For instance, eighteenth-century France was passionately interested in the religious traditions of China. This interest stemmed more or less directly from the work and observations of Jesuit missionaries in China during the previous century, but owed its existence less to any genuine concern for Chinese culture than to the belief that in China was to be found a prototype of 'natural religion', i.e. that religion, without miracle and without 'priestcraft', which the Deists had believed to be religion

---

[1] There is no comprehensive history of CSR in the English language, though various aspects of it are dealt with by e.g., L. Spence in *An Introduction to Mythology*, London, 1921, and E. E. Evans-Pritchard, *Theories of Primitive Religion*, Oxford, 1965. However, for a full account of its earlier phases, see H. Pinard de la Boullaye, *L'Etude Comparée des Religions*, Vol. I 4th ed., Paris, 1929.

in its pristine purity. In the early nineteenth century, various representatives of the Romantic movement—Emerson and Thoreau in America and Schopenhauer in Germany being typical examples—studied oriental religions to the best of their ability; but again less with a view to understanding oriental cultures than to bolstering a particular type of individualist, 'transcendental' philosophy. In neither case can one accord these studies the name 'academic'.

The turning point, as far as CSR as a scholarly discipline is concerned, came in the years immediately following the publication (in 1859) of Darwin's *Origin of Species*, as the evolutionary hypothesis came to be applied to all areas of human existence, religion not excepted. This hypothesis provided a principle on which previously amorphous bodies of miscellaneous material could be organized and classified. The *motive* for the study was already there; bodies of *material* were at hand, and growing rapidly, with the development of anthropology, archaeology, philology and kindred disciplines; now to these was added a *method*, the evolutionary method, which appeared to be the key which would unlock every door. The idea of evolution struck the late nineteenth century with the force of revelation: in the words of J. H. Moulton, 'A revelation of the Reign of Law invaded every field of thought.'[2] A new class of scholar emerged: men such as Max Müller, E. B. Tylor, J. G. Frazer, R. R. Marett and many more—analysing, with the help of the evolutionary 'key', philosophy, ritual, myth, magic, folklore and all the other ingredients of 'religion'. A new interest grew up in what might be called 'religious prehistory', or the origins of religion—religion viewed by this time not as a body of revealed doctrine but as a human function—and a rash of theories concerning religious origins broke out. Obviously this could not have happened had it not been believed that religion, in common with all other expressions of human existence, exhibits a largely unbroken evolution from lower forms to higher. J. Estlin Carpenter expressed the original dependence of CSR on the evolutionary hypothesis

[2] J. H. Moulton, *Religions and Religion*, London, 1911, p. 7.

in these words, written just before the First World War:

> It is on this great idea [evolution] that the whole study of the history of religion is now firmly established. At the foundation of all endeavours to classify the multitudinous facts which it embraces, lies the conviction that whatever may be the occasional instances of degeneration or decline, the general movement of human things advances from the cruder and less complex to the more refined and developed.[3]

So it came to be virtually axiomatic that clear stages of development could be discerned, from (using the new language of the new discipline) animatism to animism to polydaemonism to polytheism to henotheism to monotheism. In some cases it was held that the crown and culmination of the whole process was that largely undogmatic, moralistic Christianity since called, among other things, 'Liberal Protestantism'.[4]

These details are worth bearing in mind, since it is sometimes forgotten that CSR was born and raised under the optimistic auspices of evolutionary theory, and that for years it was concerned mainly with the discerning and elaboration of evolutionary patterns in the area of religion. This, for instance, goes a long way towards accounting for the traditional suspicion in which 'comparative religion' has been held by certain types of Christian, to whom the very mention of 'evolution' has been tantamount to a confession of heresy. Not that CSR was only concerned with this, of course: it was first of all necessary to gather, edit and sift masses of material from a wide variety of cultures, and this task was done with great conscientiousness, as Max Müller's series of *Sacred Books of the East* bears witness; but the passing of value judgments was never far from the minds

---

[3] J. Estlin Carpenter, *Comparative Religion*, London, 1913, p. 33.
[4] 'The Science of Religion will for the first time assign to Christianity its right place among the religions of the world; it will show for the first time fully what was meant by the fulness of time; it will restore to the whole world, in its unconscious progress towards Christianity, its true and sacred character.' F. Max Müller, *Chips from a German Workshop*, Vol. I, London, 1867, p. xx.

of the first practitioners of the new science. They might attempt to persuade themselves that the labelling of one religion as 'primitive' (or a 'survival') and another as 'higher' was a scientific procedure; in fact it was the fruit of the application of an *a priori* theory, and was therefore nowhere near as scientific as the convinced evolutionist tends to suppose.

But if we are thus disposed, with all the wisdom of hindsight, to criticize the scientific basis of 'comparative religion' as originally practised, what guarantee have we that in a few years (if not at present) someone will not turn round and accuse us of being equally unscientific? To put it as sharply as possible, is CSR a scientific discipline at all?

Certainly, CSR has always found it somewhat difficult to achieve academic respectability, not least because over the past fifty years or so its exponents have been less than unanimous when it came to trying to express the precise aims they had in view. There has been uncertainty as to whether it ought to be treated as a theological discipline or whether its place ought to be among the humanities; and there have been those who have dismissed it impatiently as merely a 'fringe activity' having no academic relevance. The root of the trouble is the question of method. Methodological uncertainty has been paraded for all to see in the variety of names the subject (allowing for the moment that it *is* a subject) has carried during its brief academic life: comparative religion, comparative religions, the science of religion (*Religionswissenschaft*), the history of religion (*Religionsgeschichte*), the history of religions, the phenomenology of religion, religious studies, and so on. 'The comparative study of religion' is perhaps a compromise and may not be ideal; but for the present it will serve our purpose.[5]

It is only in very recent years that CSR has left the university and begun to enjoy independent existence on other, less exalted, academic levels. But it is illuminating to look back to see how the universities originally stood in relation to the development of

---

[5] In America, the general tendency appears to be either to refer to the discipline as 'the history of religions', or to opt out of the semantic difficulty by resorting to the German term *Religionswissenschaft*.

CSR as a non-theological discipline. The theological faculties were, with very few exceptions, at first suspicious of what seemed to them to be illegitimate trespassing on their preserves. Some in fact still are. Most tended to look upon comparative religionists much as the landed gentry once looked upon poachers —as resourceful villains who knew the terrain extraordinarily well, but were totally lacking in respect for property. They were not able to prevent the development of the new discipline, though they did succeed in considerably retarding it in some areas.

The honour of establishing the first chair in the subject belongs to Switzerland, and the University of Geneva (1873); in Holland, the theological faculties of the four Dutch universities were separated in 1877 from the Dutch Reformed Church and turned into institutes of religious studies, each with a chair in the history of religion. In 1879 a chair was established at the Collège de France, and in 1886 the subject was introduced, in ten separate sections, in the École des Hautes Études of the Sorbonne. The Free University of Brussels appointed its first professor of the subject in 1884. In the United States, by 1895, chairs had been created at Harvard, Cornell and the University of Chicago. In Scotland, the Gifford Lectures were started in 1888, but these were concerned mainly with the philosophy of religion, and with comparative religion only secondarily, and as a matter of apologetics (a situation which appears to have persisted in Scotland to the present day).

The English universities were in a very peculiar position. On the one hand, they could boast of having some of the world's outstanding representatives of the new discipline—Max Müller, Robertson Smith, Jevons, Tylor, Lubbock, Lang, Frazer and others. But on the other hand, not one of these occupied a chair of comparative religion: they were either philologists, anthropologists, or (as in the case of Lang and Frazer) essentially free-lancers. It is true that in 1904 a chair of comparative religion was set up in the University of Manchester; but until the chair of religious studies was established a few years ago in the University of Lancaster, it remained the only one of its kind in the country.[6] Departments were set up in time at other universities, and some of the concerns of comparative religion were cared for in some cases by other chairs (for example the Spalding Professorship at Oxford), but the range and effectiveness of such centres was strictly limited. It is also worth mentioning that there were some theological colleges that did offer some teaching in the subject—Manchester and Mansfield, Oxford, spring immediately to mind, though these were not the only ones—but again, there was considerable dependence on the presence of gifted and enlightened individuals, such as, in the early days, A. M. Fairbairn and J. Estlin Carpenter.

Turning for a moment to continental Europe, the Scandinavian countries and Germany have traditionally entrusted the training of their ministers of religion to Lutheran confessional faculties of theology. In Sweden, a chair with the elaborate name of Theological Propaedeutics and Theological Encyclopaedia had been in existence in the University of Uppsala since the 1870's, and its occupants had taught some comparative religion under the aspect of Christian apologetics. In 1901 Nathan Söderblom was appointed to the chair, having received his training in the heady atmosphere of the Sorbonne, and although an expert on Iranian religion, covered more ground in the thirteen years of his professorship than most teachers would expect to cover in a lifetime, his subjects ranging from primitive religion to Catholic Modernism.[7] However, in the same year, 1901, Adolf von Harnack opposed the setting up of just such a chair in the theological faculty of the University of Berlin on the grounds that it would surely lead to the production of religious dilettantes. What Harnack said in effect was that unless you have a thorough grounding in the language and culture of a people, you cannot begin even to approach their religion with any hope

---

[6] Editor's note: Even at Lancaster the chair is in religious studies and not specifically in CSR, though the present Professor, Ninian Smart, is a CSR specialist. It should also be noted that chairs at Leeds and London include, or have included, CSR (history of religion) in their titles.

[7] See E. J. Sharpe, 'Nathan Söderblom and the Study of Religion', in Religious Studies 4, 1969, pp. 259ff.

of understanding.[8] The Christian cobbler ought, he maintained, to stick to his Biblical last, and leave other religious traditions to those who are able to deal with them in depth. The difference between these two attitudes is fundamental. Söderblom was interested in everything having to do with that universal phenomenon called (rightly or wrongly) 'religion'; Harnack mainly in the Christian tradition. For Harnack, historical scientific method was everything; for Söderblom, it was a tool, to be sharpened and polished, but ultimately to be used in the interests of a better understanding of something fundamentally and inalienably human. In his inaugural lecture he had asked:

How can any education deserving of the name avoid knowing about religion? How are we to describe and understand the history of mankind without insight into that mighty, incommensurable factor in human aspiration and the destiny of peoples which we call religion? How are we to attain to any real understanding of the deepest secrets of human life in all ages and of the great present-day conflicts and questions in the world without coming up against religion?[9]

How, indeed?

It would be tempting simply to set up these two alternative approaches as the two with which CSR is faced today; but this would be something of an over-simplification. The discipline today is not what it was at the turn of the century, and the alternatives are perhaps not quite so clear-cut as they might seem.

We have already drawn attention to the close connection which originally existed between 'comparative religion' and the evolutionary hypothesis. Now while it is no part of our intention to question the *biological* theory of evolution, increasingly of late scholars have come to question whether it

---

[8] A. von Harnack, 'Die Aufgabe der theologischen Fakultäten und die allgemeine Religionsgeschichte', in *Reden und Aufsätze*, Vol. II, Gieszen, 1906, pp. 159-187. He said, among other things: 'Weist man ihr aber nur die von Sprache und Geschichte losgelöste Religionsgeschichte zu, so verurteilt man sie zu einem heillosen Dilettantismus.' (p. 167).

[9] N. Söderblom, *Om studiet av religionen*, reprint ed., Lund, 1951, p. 15.

can be successfully applied to the area of human thought, and, in this case, to the area of religion.[10] The idea of unbroken (or, at any rate, steady) progress from lower forms to higher seems less self-evident, in the light of *inter alia* two world wars, than it once did. And as a result, the method on which CSR once rested has fallen upon evil days. The early comparative religionists have been severely criticized for their cavalier treatment of the sparse and enigmatic material which they once advanced as proof of one or another theory of the origins of religion.[11] The anthropologists in particular have been taken to task for assuming that the religions of pre-literate peoples can without more ado be equated with (to quote a popular, though inaccurate, phrase) 'stone age religion'.

Furthermore, the past sixty years have seen the breakdown of a number of academic disciplines into their constituent elements as a result of the well-known process of increasing specialization. The subject which was once called 'natural philosophy' is now studied under such varied headings as botany, chemistry, physics and zoology. Anthropology was once categorized unhesitatingly as 'the science of man', but has since divided into its constituent elements of prehistoric archaeology, linguistics, physical anthropology, social anthropology, folklore, and the rest. Similarly, the sheer weight of material which has accumulated under the general heading of comparative religion is now often broken down into the history of religion, the phenomenology of religion, the psychology of religion, the sociology of religion and the philosophy of religion (not to mention a host of auxiliary disciplines), any one of which might occupy the normal scholar for rather more than his allotted three score years and ten.

[10] See e.g. G. Widengren, 'Evolutionism and the Problem of the Origin of Religion', in *Ethnos* **10**, 1945, pp. 57ff.

[11] 'About all these broadly speaking intellectualist theories [i.e. those of Spencer, Tylor, Frazer] we must say that, if they cannot be refuted, they also cannot be sustained . . . The evolutionary stages their sponsors attempted to construct, as a means of supplying the missing evidence, may have had logical consistency, but they had no historical value.' Evans-Pritchard, *op. cit.*, p. 29.

This means in practice that the optimism which once characterized the comparative religionist has now given place to extreme caution. It has been stressed repeatedly of late, in tones reminiscent of Harnack, that no student can ever hope to cover the entire field of religion. It is simply too large and too diffuse. Moreover, to treat, say, Hinduism as representing the universal category of 'religion' is to do far less than justice to its distinctive features as an aspect of Indian culture. Each religion must, in other words, be dealt with separately, historically and scientifically, on the basis of its own primary sources and against its own specific background. And in the cultivation of such a field of study, linguistic proficiency plays a very important part indeed.

What this means in practice is that in most European universities, any name involving the word 'comparative' is firmly rejected, partly in order to make clear the extent of the break with the past that has in fact taken place. Usually the subject is there called 'the history of religion', and extreme pains are taken to emphasize that its legitimacy as a scientific discipline rests entirely on its historical method. Occasionally, an additional factor contributing to this attitude has been the position which certain faculties of theology have been forced to adopt in face of the attacks of what might be called militant secularists. Sweden is a case in point, where the very existence of university faculties of theology has been challenged repeatedly this century, and where members of those faculties have asserted their own right to full academic citizenship primarily as historians. And since the average historian finds the greatest satisfaction in the intensive cultivation of a small and circumscribed area, the tendency has been to study religion microscopically, to the virtual (though by no means complete) exclusion of theorizing concerning 'religion-as-such'. It goes without saying that this kind of university discipline presupposes that the university is first and foremost a centre of scholarship, geared primarily to the needs of its professors, lecturers and research students. In this kind of climate, undergraduates may be regarded either as a necessary evil, or as potential research students, to be taught the relevant languages and the rudiments of scientific method as quickly and painlessly as possible, against the day when they are able to put away childish things.

This is of course not the only way to teach religion in a university; and it would be possible to bring forward examples of a much wider and more comprehensive approach from many parts of the world. However, the sharpest contrast at present is perhaps to be seen in the United States. In 1901, Morris Jastrow of the University of Pennsylvania, while lamenting that so little was being done to teach religion in American schools and colleges, wrote that:

The main purposes . . . for which the study of religions should be introduced into the curriculum of American colleges, and of the higher schools on the Continent leading to the university proper, are two—as part of the equipment of a liberal education, and as a necessary adjunct for appreciating and understanding the religious needs of the present time.[12]

These words are remarkably reminiscent of Söderblom's statement of the same year; and while not all scholars would probably now want to claim that we study religion in order to understand 'the religious needs of the present time', the other motif—that of the place of religion in liberal education—is being stressed in America more strongly than ever. Take, for instance, these words of Robert Michaelsen:

Religion is a fact. It is a fact which the community of learning cannot responsibly ignore. To be sure, one can debate whether religion is phenomenon or epiphenomenon; whether religious behaviour is normal or aberrant; whether religion is *sui generis* or merely the function of something else more fundamental. These are important debates which are of significance to the study of religion and will inevitably be raised in connection with such a study. But to deny the fact of religion by ignoring it is to engage in a kind of irresponsibility which does not befit the proud heritage of the community of learning. The question, then, is not *whether* to study religion, but *how* to study it.[13]

---

[12] M. Jastrow, The Study of Religion, London, 1901, p. 364.
[13] R. Michaelson, The Scholarly Study of Religion in College and University, New Haven, 1964, p. 7.

Once more we are faced with the question of methodology. This question is at present being hotly debated in the United States, as it is in Europe, but it would probably not be too much of an exaggeration to claim that most American scholars would tend to agree with the Chicago professor Joseph M. Kitagawa, who follows Joachim Wach in demanding some 'integral understanding' of the area of religion as a whole.[14] Kitawaga has written in a recent article:

We must . . . be crystal clear concerning the basic distinction between the study of specific religions and the history of religions. We are all aware, of course, that in the popular mind the history of religions is often thought of as a convenient semantic umbrella that covers all the independent studies of specific religions. But the objective of the history of religions (*Religionswissenschaft*), in the technical sense in which we use this term, must be nothing short of scholarly inquiry into the nature and structure of the religious experience of the human race and its diverse manifestations in history.[15]

Although this is admittedly a tall order, it need not for that reason be ruled out as inacceptable in principle. However, it is questionable whether it is at all practical, as things are at present, to consider this to be part of the *teaching* function of the university, college or school. We all know that we are living in a society in which ignorance of even the basic concepts and terminology of religion is so widespread as to be almost universal, even among nominal Christians. If it were the case that university students were to come to the subject with even a modicum of accurate knowledge (which many of them, by and large, do not), then we might attempt to extend and integrate that knowledge, with the help of such disciplines as sociology, social anthropology and psychology, into something approaching a 'scholarly inquiry into the nature and structure of the religious experience of the human race'. As it is, however, it seems unlikely that we shall be in a position to adopt the grand synoptic

[14] See J. Wach, The Comparative Study of Religion, New York and London, 1958.
[15] J. M. Kitagawa, 'The Making of a Historian of Religions', in Journal of the American Academy of Religion, XXXVI/3 Sept., 1968, p. 199.

view for some time to come.

But the situation at present is anything but static. We began by mentioning the remarkable upsurge of interest in CSR which is currently taking place on both sides of the Atlantic. Over the last decade, the size of undergraduate classes at Manchester has increased by 300 to 500 per cent, and many other universities have had a similar experience. If popular demand is any criterion, CSR has 'never had it so good'. But what is to be done to satisfy this demand? It seems that we are faced with the broad alternatives of following the path of sober descriptive instruction, taking one religious area at a time under conditions of the greatest scientific stringency, or of seeking, with some at least of the Americans, for an insight into 'the nature and structure of the religious experience of the human race'.

Both alternatives, if elevated into absolute principles, are, however, beset with serious pitfalls. The 'pure' historian of religion runs the risk of losing sight of the living reality of religion in the experience of a great many human beings, and may unwittingly transmute his subject into a species of antiquarianism. The cosmic visionary may know everything about religion in general and embarrassingly little about any religion in particular; lacking the patience for detailed historical and linguistic study, he may lead his students into a 'cloud-cuckoo land' in which nothing is explicable save as inspiration or aberration. The classroom is not the place for an intense dialogue of religions, while both Christian and anti-Christian apologetics are equally illegitimate in the educational setting.

Among the various practical teaching alternatives at present open to departments of CSR or religious studies, the tendency appears to be either to emphasize the present situation of religion (with which must be reckoned the recent past), endeavouring to provide a cross-section of religious and anti-religious opinion in various parts of the world, or to work in the broad sense historically, limiting courses to certain specific religious areas which can be dealt with in a couple of hours a week. Again, neither is fully satisfactory if isolated arbitrarily from the other—in the first case because of the danger of the proliferation of shallow and undifferentiated judgments, and because those who claim to be 'contemporary' are frequently in bondage to the fairly recent past; in the second, because we are not antiquarians, and must at all costs avoid becoming departments of old wives' tales and miscellaneous exotic superstitions.

Ideally, of course, when CSR is taught, at whatever level, some attempt should be made to combine description with interpretation. But since there are diversities of gifts and inclinations, some teachers of the subject will inevitably feel more drawn to the one side than to the other, and this may place a considerable strain on a one-man department. However, we do not live in an ideal world, and we have to face up to the seriously limited time that is normally available for the teaching of CSR. And this being so, our first priority must be to inform students concerning the history and phenomenology of specific religious traditions. It may be that in another decade, when CSR is more widely accepted on the secondary level, that the universities and colleges will need to spend less time teaching students the ABC of Christianity, Hinduism, Buddhism and Islam. But for the present, this must have first call upon our teaching energies.

The question inevitably arises at this point whether and to what extent the attempt should be made to compare religions. It must be recognized, in the first place, that comparison with a view to assigning religions relative places on the evolutionary ladder is no longer an acceptable option; and that comparison with a view to demonstrating the superiority of one or other religion over all its 'competitors' is illegitimate in the framework of secular education. More seriously, there are good grounds for objecting that the comparison of religious systems *as systems* is a thoroughly unprofitable exercise, partly because excessive systematization is never in the interests of accurate understanding and may (e.g., in the case of Hinduism) promote complete misunderstanding,[16] and partly because such comparisons are

---

[16] This point has been made most forcefully by W. Cantwell Smith, in The Meaning and End of Religion, Mentor ed., New York, 1964. For instance, 'The term "Hinduism" is, in my judgment, a particularly false conceptualization, one that is conspicuously incompatible with any adequate understanding of the religious outlook of Hindus', p. 61.

always ultimately between abstractions. We may compare our *understanding* of, say, Judaism and Christianity, Vedānta and Zen Buddhism; what we are not doing is to compare these phenomena as they are in themselves. This is not, however, to say that there is no place for comparison in CSR (which would be an extreme paradox); but comparison should be between comparables, for instance phenomena such as sacrifice, iconography, prayer, music and the like. This is one of the concerns of the phenomenology of religion, and ought to be given its rightful place within the discipline.

It is doubtful, however, whether we ought to waste too much time looking for 'the origins of religion', or that we should spin too many high-flown theories concerning the nature and function of 'religion-as-such': someone will always be found to pick up this particular fallen mantle.

Nor should we let our new-found popularity go to our heads; Kitagawa, in the article to which reference has already been made, is perfectly right when he says that

> It takes a considerable amount of determination for a historian of religions in-the-making to work towards creative scholarship without succumbing to the temptation to produce instant relevance either as a pseudo-Orientalist or as a quasi-theologian.[17]

The warning is timely: there is no surer formula for instant irrelevance tomorrow than instant relevance today.

At present, CSR is mainly taught in the university setting, and a university is a centre of scholarship as well as a teaching institution. This means that university teachers of CSR, as well as producing *oeuvres de vulgarisation* (for which there has never been a better market) should constantly be hard at work both perfecting and using the tools of their trade, within their chosen field of specialist study. But we all have to recognize our limitations. We have already had occasion to speak of the increasing degree of academic specialization that has led to the breakdown of the monolithic field of comparative religion, and we have referred to the fact that no single scholar can ever hope to master

[17] Kitagawa, *op. cit.*, p. 201.

the entire field of religion. So, for instance, the scholar whose training has been in Oriental languages is unlikely to want (or be able) to concern himself at any depth with problems of philosophy; and it must be accepted that the same scholar may not be in a position both to edit and interpret, say, the *Brahma Sūtras* or the *Tao Te Ching*. There is, then, ample scope for teamwork, not only within departments, but between departments and between universities. Inter-departmental co-operation still leaves a great deal to be desired in some quarters, I am afraid, partly because of conflicting methodologies. But a scheme of inter-university co-operation has recently been launched between the universities of Lancaster, Leeds, Manchester and Newcastle, in which it is hoped that our various specialists may be able to offer short courses or groups of lectures to one another's classes.

Another area in which co-operation might well be extended is that of library resources. In a field as vast as that of CSR, no single provincial library can hope to accumulate a complete range of primary sources, texts, theses, monographs and journals. This is perhaps not so much of a burden for undergraduates, but it may constitute a serious hindrance to research projects, and it is embarrassing to have to turn potential research students away on the grounds that the relevant literature is unavailable. There is of course the Inter-Library Loan System, but this is both expensive and slow, and a comprehensive system of mutual availability might be of very great benefit indeed.

So far we have been concerned almost entirely with CSR within the framework of secular education; something must now be said about CSR in the explicitly Christian setting.

Many Christians have traditionally felt that CSR has no business to be taught in Christian institutions, perhaps because they feel, like the nineteenth-century divine, that 'there may be comparative religions, but Christianity is not one of them', or like Ronald Knox, that there is nothing like comparative religion for making a person comparatively religious. At all events, CSR has long had a bad image among Christians, particularly, though not exclusively, among Christians of the Evangelical type. An

Anglican Bishop (not an Evangelical) wrote, for instance, in 1919, that 'The comparative study of religion is . . . a new obsession of the liberal mind. We are supposed to set out in parallel columns the beliefs and customs of all known religions contemporary with, or antecedent to, Christianity, to note their similarities, and to account for them all by labelling them products of the human mind.'[18] The distortion is scarcely worth refuting; yet the image has persisted, of CSR as a curious, rationalist, eclectic discipline (if this is the right word), dedicated to the devaluation and relativization of all absolutes, the slaughter of all sacred cows, and the humanization of all religions.

But the time has long since passed when the Christian could live in the world as though other religions than Christianity did not exist; this was always a dangerous delusion, and it is doubly dangerous in today's so-called 'global village'.

So to my mind it goes without saying that every Christian student (and particularly those in training for the ministry or priesthood) should receive some instruction in at least the rudiments of non-Christian religious belief and practice, ideally on the same conditions of sympathy and (as far as possible) objectivity as those obtaining in the university. A second requirement should be a course in the history of Christian attitudes to non-Christian religions—a course, incidentally, from which many historians, Christian and non-Christian alike, might profit. This would certainly give the lie to the common misapprehension that the Christian Church has in the past refused to concern itself with other religious traditions, and it might give a more balanced picture of the history of Christian missions—a subject on which ignorance in this country is so widespread as to be almost barbaric.

Let me make it quite clear that I have no quarrel whatsoever with the attempt from the side of the Christian Church to work out a theology of confrontation with other religions; in view of the actual situation of the Church in many parts of the world, this is an imperative necessity, and methodologically, it is perfectly legitimate, provided always that it is made quite explicit

[18] F. Weston, The Christ and His Critics, London, 1920, p. 57.

on what criteria the Christian is passing judgment. But in this, theological college and secular university part company; it is a confessional concern, and I hold no brief for Christian apologetics masquerading as CSR.

There is one point, however, at which university and theological college should be motivated by a similar concern. Granted that they are not identical types of institution, and that the theological college may legitimately enter upon matters which must remain for the most part closed to the university, they share one educational ideal. No study, and certainly no religious study, can entirely overlook the question of religious presuppositions; faith is itself a basic religious presupposition (though not the only one) to which no student is altogether immune. Although there are, of course, many possible answers to the question 'What is it all for?' I am tempted to say that the study of exotic and foreign religious traditions, past and present, is of value precisely in that it enables the individual, as well as discovering something about the religious presuppositions of others, to find out something of importance about his own presuppositions. It may bring them out into the light of day—perhaps for the first time—where they can be more easily weighed in the balances. That is why it is essential that in all our enthusiasm for Hinduism and Buddhism and the rest, we should not forget that Christianity is a world religion, with its own history and its own claims. It would be the height of irresponsibility for a department of religious studies or CSR deliberately to suppress such an important tradition (or, for that matter, the humanist tradition which serves as its antithesis) merely in the mistaken belief that it was giving the customer what the customer wanted.

I want to end with one severely practical matter. Time and time again in these days one hears the lament that there is such a shortage of teachers of CSR that many ideal programmes simply cannot be put into practice. The theological courses which were mentioned are for the most part entirely impracticable, since there is no one to teach them; colleges of education are aware, almost without exception, of the need for instruction in the major non-Christian traditions, not least because of the growing immigrant population: few are able to provide such instruction, because of the shortage of qualified staff. Departments of CSR in the universities are the only ones who can do anything about this problem. It is necessary that we take our responsibilities in this regard with the utmost seriousness, both by laying firm and accurately-constructed foundations, and by discouraging students from following the attractive byways of dilettantism. It would be little short of tragic if, when the tide is running so strongly in our favour, we were to miss the opportunity of influencing the course of religious education in this country for years to come.

Dr Eric J. Sharpe is Lecturer in Comparative Religion, University of Manchester.

The Structure of the Comparative Study of Religion

Ninian Smart

Since so many different activities are clustered under the title 'comparative study of religion', it is important to make some distinctions. This essay is chiefly devoted to this task. But before settling down to this, it is useful to say a word about the position of the subject in the United Kingdom. In higher education, its most likely niche is within a syllabus of theology (divinity, etc.); and the most likely rationale is that it is important for students of Christian theology to take other religions into account. It is this situation that causes the subject to be treated as shorthand for 'the study of non-Christian religions'.

This situation is largely illogical. The study of religions should not of itself make any sharp divide between Christian and non-Christian religions. The judgment that Buddhism is the most important non-Christian religion could equally be met with the judgment that Christianity is the most important non-Buddhist religion, and so on. If there is any logic at all in the treatment of comparative study of religion as having essentially to do with non-Christian religions, it must arise out of the sense that in studying Christian theology the student is *doing* theology, i.e. Christian theology; while in studying non-Christian religions he is describing them 'scientifically'—or at any rate is not *doing* Islamic theology, etc. Even so, the logic of the distinction is not very logical; since the Christian tradition itself needs descriptive, 'scientific' treatment, even apart from the theologizing.

The distinction between *doing* theology and studying religion objectively is, however, an important one. In relation to the study of religions, one can broadly divide activities into two groups: I shall dub these the A group and the B group respectively. In the B group one is concerned with expressing, criticizing, evaluating a religious tradition, or traditions, from the standpoint of a faith (or anti-faith). Christian theology, Islamic theology, Buddhology, philosophy of religion, certain sorts of dialogue—these activities have their natural home in the B group. Comparative study of religion has its natural home in the A group: but, as we shall see, once we disentangle the variety of objective studies of religion there will be a strong motive for dropping the use of the phrase 'comparative study of religion'. A revolution in nomenclature is called for.

THE A GROUP:

1. *Histories of religions.* The histories of particular religions are in principle independent, save in so far as religions historically intertwine. While on the one hand it is possible to treat the history of the Reformation without paying attention to Buddhism or even much to Islam, there are also obvious cases of intertwining. Thus early Islam and contemporary Christianity and Judaism have to be seen in historical relationship with each other; and the history of Zoroastrianism has intertwined with post-Exilic Judaism and early Christianity. But in principle the history of a faith, or of a phase of a faith, can be described independently, and for this reason there is merit in talking of *histories* in the plural.

Of course, as any historian knows, historical explanation involves more than simple narration, and thus woven into the fabric of historical enquiry are various (usually unformalized) laws or generalizations about human behaviour, institutions, etc. Even to ascribe an action of a politician to ambition is implicitly to call upon a generalization, namely, that ambition is a motive normal in the circumstances and one which tends to issue in certain sorts of behaviour. Likewise, in concentrating upon religious aspects of an historical epoch, the historian of religions may call upon cross-cultural generalizations. This itself presupposes the possibility of a typology. Thus we can classify different actions as being motivated by ambition (psychological typology); while in the more directly religious context, one can make use of types such as *prophecy, rites of passage, sacramental, prayer, sect,* etc. This brings us to the second activity falling under the A group.

2. *Typological phenomenology of religion.* The variations in breadth and depth manifested by scholars working in this field are great. As an example of an intendedly comprehensive typology, one can cite Gerardus van der Leeuw's *Religion in Essence and Manifestation.* Rudolf Otto's *The Idea of the Holy* is a case where the main emphasis is upon religious experience (in addition Otto appends to the pure phenomenology a philosophical theory about the *validity* of religious experience). On a narrower band is the same author's *Mysticism East and West,* dealing with the analogies between the doctrines and experiences of Eckhart and Sankara. Sometimes works which at first sight appear to be simply typological and descriptive in intent may have an apologetic foundation, as in R. C. Zaehner's *Mysticism Sacred and Profane*—such a work hovers uncertainly between the A and the B group. This by itself is no fatal criticism, provided an author knows what he is doing. Since there is a great deal of confusion about the aims of the comparative study of religion, this is not always a wise assumption to make.

It may be noted that the comparative descriptive task involved in typological phenomenology must be sensitively undertaken, with due regard to the principle of intentionality—namely to the principle that in human experience and activity the way the person involved sees his activity or experience is an important part of the description.

Some of the doubts liable to be expressed about the validity of the phenomenological, comparative approach are caused by the principle of intentionality. How can it be respected and at the same time generalization preserved? First, it might be objected, every religious experience, institution, etc., is historically particular, and thus particular in regard to the intentions of the participants. Second, the participant may not see his action as the phenomenologist does. For example, the latter may see the *lingam* as a fertility symbol, or some of Charles Wesley's hymns as fervent expressions of *bhakti* religion: but these are not the terms which the participants might want to use (and indeed could react against them). Despite these objections, however, sufficiently sensitive work in phenomenology has been achieved to justify it. As for the first objection, it merely draws attention to the fact that there are particularities, and phenomenology cannot hope to capture them all. Likewise, though it is true to say that the tree in my garden is an oak, it has its own special shape. As for the second objection, this merely draws our attention to the way in which the advance of the human sciences makes a difference to human consciousness itself. Once people become sensitively aware of parallels between different religions, including their own, they will inevitably come to look upon their own faith in a different way. In brief, phenomenology has its repercussions on the phenomena. Similar situations have arisen in psychology and sociology (consider the way in which the idea of the Freudian slip has affected the manner in which educated people look upon their own verbal errors).

We have already seen that sometimes phenomenology has a hidden apologetic basis (and to that extent is no longer pure phenomenology). It can also have a different sort of debatable basis. Thus the work of C. G. Jung on the *mandala*, for example, is highly charged with Jungian theory; and much of Eliade's later work is likewise affected about a general theory of human existence and historical consciousness. There is some merit in separating such work out from purely typological approaches (pure comparison and contrast, as it were). This leads us then to the third activity in the A group:

3. *Speculative phenomenology of religion.* Naturally, sometimes such a speculative approach has a relationship to apologetics, since it tends to be informed with a general *Weltanschauung*, which may be favourable or unfavourable to a particular faith-stance. The materials may tend to be arranged according to a preconceived pattern, itself incapable of being thoroughly insulated from theological (or anti-theological)

assumptions. It might be replied that the study of religion can *never* achieve such a virgin objectivity as I have implicitly been arguing for. However, much harm has been done by theological subjectivism in the field of the study of religion, for it can too easily be used as a licence for unfairness, lack of clarity and the tendency to be guided by apologetic considerations rather than by respect for the facts viewed relatively dispassionately. (Contrarily, the phenomenology of religion can be distorted by over-rationalistic approaches, e.g. to the phenomenon of myth.)

The classification of religious experiences, institutions, doctrines, etc., is, however, only laying the groundwork for deeper explorations. That it is relevant to questions of religious truth (in the B group) goes without saying. But it is also central to the enterprise of explanatory theories of religion, as in psychology of religion, sociology and anthropology.

4. *Sociology of religion, anthropology.* From an explanatory and theoretical point of view, in the social sciences, religion is of obvious and great importance. Thus much of the central work in sociology and anthropology—the work, for instance, of Max Weber, Emile Durkheim and Claude Levi-Strauss—has concerned the role of religious institutions in society. It will, moreover, readily be agreed that at least part of the explanation of a given style of belief, as institutionalized in a religious structure, has to do with the social forces at work in the society in which the community is embedded. To this extent, sociological (and anthropological) explanations of religious phenomena are in order. Conversely, there are dynamic elements in a religious tradition which help to shape a given social milieu. In both sorts of interplay historians and sociologists are seeking explanations. Since a main feature of scientific enquiry is the search for explanations, there are good reasons to dub this sort of investigation of religion as 'scientific'. It is true that, as to some extent in other branches of science, a given theory or set of explanations may be *debatable*—so that one should avoid the vulgar equation of 'scientific' with 'well-established'; but the main rationale of calling a given pursuit 'scientific' is that it is in broad terms committed to a certain methodology. It is not that

the social sciences need to ape the physical sciences in detail; rather it is that they seek explanatory theories, tested against the data as far as possible.

But here a problem arises. One cannot put history in a test-tube; nor can one get a society inside a laboratory, to perform experiments on it. This is a severe limitation upon the experimental aspect of the social sciences (and indeed upon psychology in so far as it is intertwined with sociology and anthropology). The best that can be done is to test hypotheses against the data supplied in a variety of independent living societies and in their histories. This was a point seen with the greatest clarity by Max Weber. Hence his studies of Indian, Chinese and other religions, in conjunction with his work on the spirit of capitalism in relation to the Protestant ethic. Comparative, cross-cultural testing functions as a form of experiment and a check on theories. Thus it is of the essence of sociology, if it is to become scientifically validated, that it is comparative. In regard to religion, therefore, typological phenomenology must play a crucial role, for it supplies an ordering of the data. Consider, for instance, the function of the concept of *prophecy* in Weber—and consider also the question of whether from a phenomenological and historical point of view Weber's concept is justly delineated and applied.

Similar remarks apply, naturally enough, to work in the psychology of religion.

5. *The psychology of religion.* There is a clear overlap between this and the foregoing category. The overlap can be put in the following way. In so far as psychology has to do with the explanation of individual actions, occurrences, etc., it has to take cognizance of the norms operative for society in a given milieu. For instance, in a tribe where men and women go around naked, no special explanation is called for if a given individual is walking around on a sunny morning wearing no clothes. But the observation of a man walking down Piccadilly with no clothes on might call for some investigation. It could be that he is doing it for a bet or as a protest; but there is *prima facie* evidence from the *social* situation, as well as from his action, that some special

psychological explanation of his action needs investigating. Hence it is hard to disentangle psychological and sociological approaches to human behaviour, including of course religious behaviour.

It is thus no surprise that part of the enterprise known as psychology of religion is cross-cultural, for the same reason that sociology needs to be comparative if it is to be as fully experimental as the subject-matter allows. For instance, the Freudian account of the genesis of the Father-figure in religion needs to be tested not only against the historical evidence in the Judaeo-Christian tradition, but also by reference to *prima facie* counter-examples in other cultures (e.g. Theravada Buddhism, which has no special place for a supreme personal God).

Some concluding remarks about the A *group.* The delineation of these categories of descriptive, scientific studies of religion appears at first sight to leave on one side what is likely to be in the forefront of many people's minds—the task, simply, of *understanding* a given religious tradition, whether one's own or another's. Surely, it will be said, a prime task of the comparative study of religion is to give insight into particular faiths—not just historically, not just phenomenologically, not just sociologically and not just psychologically. And insight into another faith can be an important element in promoting international, inter-community understanding, etc.

However, this objection misses the mark: for it is implicit in the notion that one can study (and come to understand) the history of a particular faith (A 1 above) that one can come to terms with a cross-section—a temporal cross-section—of that faith. For example, one can come to terms with *contemporary* Islam. But to see Islam in the round, one must not merely know something of its past, above all the past that enters into the intentions and consciousness of contemporary Muslims; but also about its social institutions and its psychology. To some degree also one is bound here to be engaged in typological phenomenology; for the understanding of, for example, Muslim prayer is already to see it under a category of religious activity. It is moreover no bad thing if comparisons and contrasts between one's own tradition and another are made explicit, for it is by bringing them to the surface that one can begin to see another faith in its own right, by transcending what might otherwise be inept, comparative presuppositions about it.

It is, however, worth stressing that a religion is organic—interwoven of a complex of doctrinal, mythical, ethical, experiential, ritual and institutional parts. It is artificial to abstract from a faith, therefore; nor one must lose sight of the principle of intentionality. If a faith is organic, so likewise is the intentionality, the consciousness, of those participating in it. It would thus be illusory to suppose that one may exhaust the meaning of a faith by typological phenomenology as applied to it. The historical aspect of the study of a faith safeguards, fortunately, against this tendency, and brings out the uniqueness of a faith (of every faith, indeed).

A final remark about group A: since the process of comparison is simply the activity of doing phenomenology (unless apologetic and other B-group interests obtrude), there is no special need to retain the clumsy title 'comparative study of religion'. Indeed, in view of the interlocking character of history, phenomenology, sociology and so on, it is probably simplest to talk about the study of religion. Since, however, that term might be most naturally used to cover both A and B activities, one might particularize somewhat and use the term 'scientific study of religion'.

This is probably the best course, provided it is remembered that much of it can be debatable and some of it speculative, so that there may be interactions with activities properly falling under the B group, such as the philosophy of religion.

THE B GROUP:

1. *Theologies.* A main task of the religious intellectual is to elaborate or develop a theology expressing his own and the community's faith. The need for a theology is itself often the product of changing social and cultural patterns, which bring out the need for a continued re-statement of the traditional faith. The theologian in systematizing or otherwise intellectually

expressing the core of faith typically also is expressing value judgments, since a faith has ethical and social consequences. Thus the taking up of a theological stance is also taking up a value-stance: it is not just theory, it recommends practice.

Though it is common in this country to identify theology with Christian theology, it is transparent that there can be analogous activities such as Islamic theology, Hindu theology, etc. Historically, it is true that the term 'theology' does not always fit too snugly e.g. in Buddhism ('Buddhist theology' is a paradox when there is scarcely a Theos). But this is a merely terminological difficulty. It is quite clear that Swami Vivekananda (for instance) was theologizing from a Hindu, or from one Hindu point of view, just as Karl Barth was expressing a Christian point of view.

An important feature, in these latter days of increased mutual awareness as between the religions, of a theology is theologizing about other religions. In the West it has sometimes been that the Christian theology of other religions has been mixed up with the comparative study of religion. Obviously, descriptive and phenomenological studies are a necessary prerequisite of a sensitive theology of other religions; but the task of theologizing is different from that of describing, etc. It is worth noting in addition that as it is legitimate for the Christian theologian to try to make sense, from the standpoint of the Christian faith, of non-Christian religions, so likewise is it for the Hindu to try to make sense, from the Hindu point of view, of Christianity and other non-Hindu traditions.

For the sake of completeness, it is useful here (if again a little paradoxical) to count atheistic doctrine as a kind of theology. The atheist too is taking up a standpoint, and from it he judges the religions. It is in this connection unwise to treat the non-theological character of sociology of religion, for example, as signifying a sort of implicit atheism. It is easy to think that because a scientific study of religion does not start from faith or from appeal to authority, etc., it is against faith. The illusion is indeed fostered by the fact that sometimes atheistic doctrine creeps into supposedly scientific studies—there is an important way in which Freudian theory has incorporated a kind of atheistic critique of religion. But strictly it is not the function of the sociological or psychological study of religion to determine, off its own bat, the truth or otherwise of faith.

Now it is clear that sometimes a theology comes into conflict with a science, as happened notoriously over evolutionary theory; and so in principle a theology could come into conflict with phenomenology, sociology or psychology. All I am here wishing to point out is that there is no *a priori* necessity for such a conflict. Moreover, any phenomenology, sociology or psychology which does not take seriously the particular contents of a faith or faiths is liable to be bad science. Distortions can occur both because of uncritical theological zeal and because of uncritical rationalism.

However, the intellectual future is always somewhat unpredictable. The future relations between theologies and the social and other sciences cannot be laid down in advance. Here there are liable to be boundary disputes, to be settled largely by philosophical considerations. This is one way in which theology cannot be partitioned off absolutely from the philosophy of religion. And since the philosophy of religion moves in debated territory, it is ever liable to issue forth in appraisals of truth-claims in Christian and other theologies (including atheistic). In this way it is not a neutral enterprise, and can thus form a second category in the B group.

2. *Philosophy of religion.* Though I have said that philosophy is not neutral, in one aspect it can be, namely in the analysis of religious language, if this is undertaken without hidden apologetic aims. However, since natural theology, philosophical theology and the settling of boundary disputes are likely to remain central to philosophizing about religion, it is more realistic to place the subject in the B group rather than in the A group. Indeed, philosophy of religion in some of its manifestations falls directly under the head of apologetics, and thus is a kind of theologizing.

It is worth noting that great gains can come to the analysis of religious concepts through use of phenomenology and histories of religions. It is unfortunate that much analysis has been pursued in a non-comparative manner. Generalizations about religious language as being essentially parabolic (for instance) would not so easily stand up to the evidence if that evidence included a consideration of some of the major non-Christian faiths. But also the existence of differing world faiths brings out the need to consider the question of criteria of truth in religion in this wider context. This is a task as yet severely under-developed. It is not, incidentally, simply to be equated with so-called 'dialogue' between religions, as will be shown below. The question of criteria in some ways goes much deeper than dialogue.

3. *Dialogue between religions.* It happens that at the present time dialogue is a fashionable activity, and this is a good thing, for it signifies that men of different faiths are happy to enter into conversation and exchange. It is the starting-point of a wider ecumenicity, necessary if the scars of inter-religious conflict are to be healed and necessary too for the burial of European ideas of cultural-religious superiority. However, what does dialogue in essence amount to? At one level it is simply a means to mutual *understanding.* In this respect it is a personalized way of doing history of religions and phenomenology. But at another level it is part of the process of mutual theological adjustment, and the attempt to work out new faith-perspectives. At this level, it is a kind of polycentric theologizing. Thus there is reason to place this activity in the B group, even if, as we have said, part of what goes on is personalized history and phenomenology.

CONCLUSION

I have attempted in this essay to sketch out some of the more important intellectual activities falling under the study of religion. The comparative study of religion (so-called—for as we saw there may be merit in dropping this title) is most centrally concerned with histories of religions and the phenomenology of religion. It thereby provides substance for the sociology and psychology of religion, and is a necessary element if anyone wants to go on to theologize or philosophize about other religions and about the criteria of truth in religion. But the comparative study of religion at its heart is more concerned with *understanding* than with adjudicating. It is not a sort of theology and does not begin from a faith or an anti-faith stance. In this sense it is 'objective' (or at least it is not subjective).

Naturally there are ways in which the activities of the A group and those of the B group interact. It is unlikely that the study of religion can ever be fully rich without including both sorts of approaches; but in this country the B group activities especially have tended to be dominant and the world of the A group left as rather marginal. This is a great pity, not only because educationally the field of the study of religion has been unduly restricted, but also because our understanding of religion and religions at the A level is still in a relatively primitive state. Phenomenology, sociology and psychology are relatively recent growths. The latter part of the twentieth century is a time yet early in the history of these endeavours; there is much indeed to be learned in the future.

Fortunately for the study of religion, the shrunken world of jets and the mutual presence to one another of men of differing faiths and ideologies make it plain to see that the subject is well worth investing brains and effort in. And hearts—for only by finding how things feel to other men can we claim to have gone far in exploring the content of faiths.

Though it has not, save by implication, been a theme of this essay, it is worth finally reflecting that non-religious ideologies themselves in some degree play in the same league as religious faiths. Thus laterally the study of religion needs to branch out towards the study of 'non-religion'. Perhaps the world of Mao Tse-Tung can be understood by some of the approaches being developed in the study of religion.

Professor Ninian Smart is Professor of Religious Studies, University of Lancaster.

The Comparative Study of Religion in West Riding Schools[1]

JOHN R. HINNELLS

It is often said that there is a growing interest in the educational world in the comparative study of religion.[2] Yet apart from the increasing numbers of students taking the subject at various universities, no factual evidence to support this belief has been adduced. A survey was therefore undertaken in order to put a quantitive assessment on this vague feeling, suspicion or 'hunch', by doing some counting at the heart of the educational system, the schools.

This survey was essentially a pilot scheme, and the conclusions reached must be seen in this exploratory context as an attempt to identify trends of thought. A random survey was made of one hundred secondary schools in the West Riding, a questionnaire being sent to the head-teacher and RE specialist in each school. Replies were received from fifty-two schools, although both members of staff did not reply from every school. Thirty-three

[1] I wish to stress my indebtedness to a number of people; Mr D. G. Butler of Walbottle Grammar school, Northumberland; the late Dr A. Mackenzie of Northern Counties College of Education, Newcastle; Mr G. Smith, of Northumberland College of Education and members of an industrial market research team who, unfortunately, wish to remain anonymous. All of them spent many hours discussing the form of the questionnaire and the results. Without their help this survey could not have been made. I would also like to thank Sir Alec Clegg, the Director of Education for the West Riding for permission to undertake the survey, and the Revd. A. Loosemore, Religious Education Advisor in the West Riding for his co-operation, and finally the Dept of Adult Education, Newcastle University for help in producing and circulating the questionnaire.

[2] See the Introduction, and Dr Sharpe's article, this volume, pp. ix and 1.

TABLE 1. The sample of schools covered in the questionnaire.[a]

a. *Sizes of schools*

under 500 pupils		15
500-700	„	12
700-1000	„	17
over 1000	„	6
	Total	50

b. *Nature of Schools*

co-educational	42
boys	5
girls	3
Total	50

c. *Denominational Schools*   2

d. *Number of qualified RE Specialists*[b]

Specialists	Schools
nil	7
1	12
2	15
3	9
4	4
5	1
10	1
Total	49

e. *Schools with immigrant children*

more than 20	3
less than 20	13
none	34
Total	50

f. *Schools with sixth forms*[b]   24
   without sixth forms   26

Total	50

Notes:

a. Two schools did not supply any of the above details.
b. One school queried the meaning of 'qualified' and did not answer this question.

head-teachers and forty RE specialists returned completed questionnaires giving a total of seventy-three respondents. Table 1 shows the sample of schools that was obtained.

For the purposes of the questionnaire the comparative study of religion was defined as 'the study of the history, literature and beliefs of the major non-Christian religions'. Because the title is rather a long one it was abbreviated to CSR, a practice which will be continued here. The questionnaire had five sections:

1. A factual question; is the subject already taught in your school, if so, how much and included in which subject?
2. What do you consider the value of CSR in schools to be?
3. What do you consider the educational and practical problems involved in the subject to be?
4. To what age group, if any, are the various topics listed suitable?
5. What are your views on CSR as an examination subject?

From Table 2 it can be seen that CSR was taught to a greater or lesser degree in 88% of the schools which replied, virtually always as part of RE (Table 3). This very high percentage has two important implications, the first and obvious one, is that the subject is much more widely taught than many realize. The second is that the respondents had some idea of the subject, thus making their answers all the more valuable. A word of caution needs to be given at this point, however. In replying that 'a little' CSR is taught in the school some respondents indicate that it plays an almost negligible role in the syllabus. Thus one teacher writes that it has value 'as a supplement to geography' and one wonders just how little 'a little' is.

Turning to the values the respondents saw in the subject, of the seventy-three scripts, only twelve, or 16%, thought that there was little or no value in the subject. One head-teacher gave the opinion that 'I cannot see that CSR is in any major respect relevant to the lives and experience of the majority of people in this country.' An RE teacher thought that 'much more realistic alternatives would be Humanism and Existentialism'. Since this

TABLE 2. Level of CSR teaching in schools

Question: *Is CSR taught in your school?*

in depth?	6
a little?	40
not at all?	6
Total	52

TABLE 3. Position of CSR in Curriculum

Question: *Is CSR taught as a subject in its own right?*

Is CSR taught as a subject in its own right?	1
Or as part of R.E.?	40
History?	4
Geography?	3
Social Studies?	0
General Studies?	3
English?	1
Art?	1

Allowing for the fact that 6 do not have the subject at all it will be deduced from the above that some schools include CSR in more than one subject. Four schools only have the subject outside RE altogether, one has the subject in its own right, two in general studies only, one in history only.

TABLE 4. The Value of CSR.

Question: *What value do you think CSR has, or might have, in schools?*

Leads to greater understanding and tolerance[a]	27
Helps towards the understanding of the religious phenomenon	16
Helps towards the solution of the immigrant problem	13
Extends the pupil's educational horizons[a]	10
Valuable as pure knowledge	7
Helps the pupil to understand Christianity	7
Justifies the Christian faith	4
Provokes thought	4
Deepens pupil's understanding of man	3
Little or no value	11[b]

Notes: a. logically and explicitly in many scripts these two categories are very close and almost warrant conflation.

b. Since many respondents noted more than one value these totals exceed the number of respondents. For other values by very few respondents see Table 9.

is the view of a small minority (16%), however, attention will be concentrated on the values that were noted (Table 4). They stressed its educational value in increasing tolerance and understanding, and in broadening the pupil's educational horizons. The religious value of the subject was seen as secondary to the wider implications. These views can best be expressed by quoting a number of the replies. One RE specialist wrote:

I believe that CSR should help to banish some of the intolerance to 'other' religious groups which arises through ignorance of their beliefs and practices.

Another said:

to understand other people's beliefs and ideals, and to appreciate their values, contributes to the better communications between all races and indirectly to the peace which we seek among nations.

A teacher who stressed the widest possible context for the teaching of CSR answered:

Religion is obviously an aspect or part of human society as we know it (it is therefore part of 'human geography' and 'social studies') and should be included in a balanced syllabus. The value is in its contribution to the understanding of human society, customs, institutions and their roots in human needs.

This understanding of man and the increase in tolerance was applied to the immigrant problem by a number of respondents, although in view of the mass of material on this problem on radio, television and in the papers it is surprising how few stressed this particular point. Only thirteen scripts specifically related CSR to the immigrant problem. One head-teacher who did so, commented that CSR helps the pupil 'to understand the other person's point of view, [it is] a means of helping to banish prejudices which might and do exist in a multi-racial society.' Three teachers went much further than this and suggested that CSR should be taught only in areas where there is a sizeable immigrant community.

As Table 4 shows, many also stressed the religious value of CSR, and in particular it was emphasized that it would make the pupil aware of the universal religious quest of man. Thus one teacher suggested that it promotes 'an awareness of the range and depth of mankind's religious experience'. Another believes that CSR has 'an essential part to play in the provision of a basic understanding of the religious consciousness and of the history of ideas.' One man teaching the subject in depth comments: 'CSR relates closely to the new open-thinking amongst Christian theologians and opens up profitable lines of debate on ideas about God and ethics in general.'

Eleven respondents thought that CSR would help the pupil's own understanding of, or belief in, Christianity. So one wrote:

It sets the doctrines and ethos of Christianity into a world context, and leads to a broader appreciation of the Christian heritage.

Another teacher wrote:

[Its value lies] in the establishing of the fact among children, of the deep universal spirit of worship common to all men: the growing awareness that all peoples of the earth, with their various religions form one community: the values of goodness and truth in the searchings of great men of great faiths which can help us in our own questing into the mysteries of life and death, sin and sorrow, growth and decay: a deeper appreciation of Christ as the fulfilment of all these religions also.

Four respondents also believed that CSR would justify the Christian faith in the eyes of the pupils. Thus one head-teacher wrote that it 'might illumine the merits of Christianity vis-à-vis the other religions'. One teacher commented that it 'might show the superior value, standards and power of real Christianity'.

This attitude to CSR as an aid to religious faith is much more common among RE specialists than among head-teachers (two head-teachers, and nine RE specialists held this view).

Turning to the future of the subject, the replies were divided into those who wanted to see the subject expand in the school syllabus (hereafter designated 'Expansionists'), and those who wanted to see it left in the syllabus but only as a small part of it (hereafter designated 'Leavers').[3] Table 5 shows that respondents were fairly equally divided on this question, with a small majority in favour of its expansion. But with only seven scripts (10%) arguing that it should have no place in the syllabus there is a much greater demand for CSR than one might expect.

Those respondents who wanted to see CSR have a place in the syllabus were then asked what they considered to be the most suitable material for the different age groups within the secondary age range. The figures are given in Table 6, and speak for themselves. Briefly, respondents thought that the lives of the great teachers was the most suitable material for the 11-13 age range, although many thought that the way of life inculcated by the various religions and the forms of worship were also suitable. For the 14-16 age range the ways of life and the ways of worship were thought the most suitable, and for the 16-18 group the stress was on the doctrines of the various religions. It is noteworthy that 66% of the respondents believe CSR to be a suitable subject for use throughout the school, rather than a subject to be reserved for the sixth form. Five replies suggested that 'ways of life' should be a theme throughout the whole school syllabus.

If CSR is to be given a significant place within the school syllabus then the next obvious question is its place within the examination system. The figures in Table 7 show that there is a great deal of support for CSR as an examination subject in some form or other. The objections that are raised are that religion generally, including Christianity, is not a subject suitable for examinations. So one head-teacher wrote:

[3] Although rather ugly these terms have been adopted for the sake of brevity since they are clear and less emotive than, for example, 'Conservatives' and 'Liberals'! They have, however, a further unfortunate effect. Within the category of 'Leavers' are a variety of shades of enthusiasm for CSR, covering both the script which refers to the subject as 'a supplement to geography etc.' and the more enthusiastic script which sees the value of CSR in contributing to 'better communications between all races and indirectly to the peace which we seek among nations'. Clearly any further survey which attempts to quantify attitudes more widely and more precisely must cater for further sub-groups. Naturally those who wanted to see the subject 'left in depth' have been excluded from the figures for the 'Leavers'.

Religion has to do with attitudes and faith. I am not particularly happy about regarding RE in any form as an examinable subject.

Another commented that it is too personal, too complex a subject to be examined. Some, however, thought that CSR was a special case for not being examined. One teacher objected that 'it would have to be doctrinal, and this is not done for Christianity'. He did not explain why it would have to be doctrinal, and it is difficult to see why it should be so. One head-teacher offered an obviously heartfelt plea: 'Certainly not, let us not have theologians!'

At one school there is obviously some disagreement. The teacher suggested that taking CSR as an examination subject would help to broaden the subject, and give pupils a deeper insight into 'our own religion'. The headmistress obviously read this, and added to her own questionnaire the comment:

A deeper insight into our own is gained by dedicating oneself more to our own, see I Chron. 4:10!

The general feeling, however, was summed up by a teacher who wrote:

Insofar as we live in an external-examination orientated education system, CSR has a strong claim to be recognized by having GCE or CSE papers of its own.

In the same vein a head-teacher wrote:

There is no reason (why CSR should not be accepted as an examination subject) if scripture knowledge is accepted.

Five respondents suggested that an examination in CSR would be of particular benefit in immigrant areas. Thus, although there was some difference over the form the examination should take (whole or part of CSE, GCE 'O' or 'A' level, see Table 7) there was a clear and definite majority in favour of CSR being incorporated into the examination system.

TABLE 5. The Future of CSR.

Question: *Would you like to see CSR in your school?*

	Headteacher	RE Specialists	Totals
Left as it is *a*) at a little?	13	15	28
b) in depth?	3	2	5
c) left out altogether?	1	6	7
Reduced or withdrawn?	0	0	0
Introduced?	2	0	2
Expanded?	14	17[a]	31
	33	40	73

Note: *a*. Two RE specialists who taught the subject in depth still wanted to expand.

TABLE 6. The Suitability of material.

Question: *To which of the age groups, shown below, would you teach the topics suggested?*

11-13 *age group*	Headteachers	RE Specialists	Totals
Ways of worship	10	11	21
Way of life	12	13	25
Great teachers	17	11	28
Doctrine	1	1	2
14-16 age group			
Ways of worship	18	27	45
Way of life	22	23	45
Great teachers	17	21	38
Doctrine	9	9	18
16-18 age group			
Ways of worship	12	14	26
Way of life	11	18	29
Great teachers	8	15	23
Doctrine	20	27	47

Those who consider that it should be taught only:

after the age of 14	6	10	16
in sixth form	3	6	9

The increase in figures in the 14-16 age group is due to three factors:

a) As compared with the 16-18 age group, the fact that many schools (see Table 1) do not have a sixth form.

b) As compared with the 11-13 age group, the fact that a number do not believe the subject taught until the age of 14.

c) Sixteen respondents believed that CSR should be introduced gradually over the three stages noted.

It should also be noted that 12 respondents did not accept the categories given.

Four conclusions can be drawn from these replies as to the place and value of CSR in schools. First, there was a definite affirmative to its inclusion and expansion in the school syllabus. Second, its value was seen in the widest possible educational context, and not only as a part of RE (though that was where it was usually included on the timetable). Third, it is thought of as a subject to be taught throughout the school. Last, a majority of teachers support the inclusion of CSR into the examination system.

Objections to the inclusion of the subject in the school syllabus were raised, however, and problems were envisaged. Attention will now be given to these. The questionnaire distinguished between two sets of problems, theoretical and practical. It is here that a difference between the views of head-teachers and RE specialists begins to emerge. Twice the number of RE specialists compared with head-teachers said that the main problem with the introduction of CSR would be that Christianity would suffer (Table 8). This was, in fact, their main objection to the subject. Part of the fear was that time would be taken from Christianity. It was repeatedly stated that even after five years at secondary school the pupils did not understand what Christianity is. So one teacher wrote that 'time "wasted" on CSR might be more profitably spent on Christianity'. Another teacher expressed the view that 'the teaching of Christianity falls more and more on the schools: to find additional time for CSR would presumably take time from time allowed to Christianity'. But half of the answers did not express fears on the time question so much as fears that it would destroy faith. One teacher was worried in case the pupil, seeing the differences between religions should lose faith in 'all the truth revealed'.

A head-teacher wrote:

I would wish that children would grow up without any sort of questioning about Christianity being inextricably interwoven into the fabric of our society. Insofar as CSR draws attention to other ways of religious thought I consider it might be dangerous for children of too tender years.

That head-teacher then goes on to suggest that CSR should

TABLE 7. CSR as an examination subject.

Question: *What are your feelings about CSR forming all or part of a paper in an external examination (CSE, GCE, 'O' or 'A' level)?*

	Headteachers	RE Specialists	Totals
CSE, whole paper	0	0	0
part of a paper	5	10	15
GCE 'O' level, whole paper	2	3	5
part of a paper	1	2	3
GCE 'A' level, whole paper	10	6	16
part of a paper	1	7	8
Those who gave simple affirmative without specifying form of examination	10	8	18

Note: since some respondents noted more than one form of examination these totals exceed the number of those in favour of CSR as an examination subject.)

	Headteachers	RE Specialists	Totals
Total of those who accepted CSR as an examination in some form or other	24	30	54
Those who rejected CSR as an examination subject	9	10	19
Totals	33	40	73

TABLE 8. Educational Problems involved in CSR.

Question: *What disadvantages and/or danger might arise, in your opinion, from CSR in schools?*[a]

	Headteachers	RE Specialists	Totals
CSR will hamper the teaching of Christianty	6	12	18
It is likely the subject will be taught superficially	6	4	10
May cause confusion in the child's mind	2	6	8
Likely to be taught badly	3	3	6
Danger of emphasizing racial differences	1	2	3
Skirts the real issues	1	1	2
Boring	0	2	2
May reduce moral standards	1	0	1
Provides no foundation for individual belief	1	0	1
	21	30	51
No significant educational problems	17	10	27

Notes: *a* This Table lists only educational, or theoretical problems, Tables 11 and 12 deal with practical problems.
b of all 'theoretical' problems raised against CSR, 59% from RE Specialists, 41% from headteachers.

be taught in the sixth form, so that he does see it having a small role in the school syllabus. One head-teacher expressed particularly clearly the fears of several. He wrote:

Other religions could easily appear more attractive than the version of Christianity the pupil has grown up with [and he may then] adopt a lesser faith.

Another declared:

As a convinced Christian knowing the power of the Lord Jesus Christ my attitude to other faiths could be expressed in terms of Isaiah 44:8 & 9 [which reads:
'Is there a god besides me?'
There is no rock: I know not any
All who make idols are nothing, and the things they delight in do not profit; their witnesses neither see nor know, that they may be put to shame.]

One point ought to be made clear, only one script argued that Christianity should occupy the main place in the RE syllabus on the grounds that it is the faith most encountered by the pupils in their own environment, the others justified it in the terms quoted above, that is on apologetic and not on educational grounds. Such apologetic motives were not confined to the 'Leavers', two of the 'Expansionists' based their arguments on apologetic grounds also. It does seem, therefore, that CSR is thought to be such a threat because a number of RE specialists are committed to the propagation of Christianity for religious rather than educational reasons. They regard their teaching in a vocational and evangelistic context rather than purely as a scientific study of the Christian heritage as an historic force which has helped to shape our culture. It also seems that these teachers have little knowledge of CSR and fear the unknown. This is clearly a fact which needs to be taken into consideration by anyone seeking to expand the teaching of the subject in schools.

One interesting difference which emerged between 'Expansionists' and 'Leavers' was in the values attributed to the two groups to CSR, and in the difficulties they envisaged. Whereas the 'Expansionists' were reasonably united in the values they attributed to the subject, essentially the understanding of others, the 'Leavers' produced what might be labelled a 'hotch-potch' of values. Eleven values were noted by 'Expansionists' seventeen by 'Leavers' (see Table 9). The same observations can also be made with regard to the problems noted by the two groups. The 'Leavers' stressed that CSR would detract from Christianity whereas the 'Expansionists' on the whole saw no educational problems (Table 10).[4]

The main objections on educational grounds were the danger of confusing the pupil with the vastness of the material, or going to the opposite extreme and giving pupils a version over-simplified to the point of distortion (Table 10). One teacher suggested that a danger would be that 'in a rather conservative area, there is an unwillingness to consider other practices as rational and not just "weird".'

One teacher, a 'Leaver', suggested that 'to concentrate too much on the various teachings can be very boring to the children.' The view of a teacher who thought that the subject should have no place in the school syllabus was that

It is difficult to teach more than the basic factual outline of different religions, without being able to participate in them. Religion cannot be separated from its social environment (e.g., Hinduism) subsequently to do justice to these religions is impossible because of the complexity of the subject.

Three respondents were concerned that CSR might emphasize the racial differences. Despite these doubts and objections, however, nearly half the respondents saw no educational problems in the teaching of CSR, none, that is, that are peculiar to the subject. Thus one head-teacher wrote: 'as with any other subject the success would depend on the teacher'.

---

[4] This statement must not be confused with that on p. 46f. where it is said that it is the 'Expansionists' who are aware of practical problems. The point here is the consideration of theoretical or educational problems.

TABLE 9. Analysis of Table 4.

Question: *What value do you think CSR has?*

	'Leavers' (at little)	Leave out	Leave in depth	Introd-uction	Expan-sion	Expansion from depth
Increase tolerance and understanding	9	0	2	1	13	2
understanding of religious phenomenon	2	0	1	1	11	1
help towards solution of immigrant problem	6	0	0	0	6	1
extends the pupil's educational horizons	2	0	1	0	7	0
valuable as pure knowledge	5	0	0	0	2	0
helps pupil understand Christianity	1	0	1	0	5	0
justifies the Christian faith	2	0	0	0	2	0
provokes thought	2	0	0	1	1	0
deepens the pupil's understanding of man	0	0	1	0	1	1
little or no value	5	5	0	1	0	0

Notes: a. Further values noted, all by 'Leavers' only: enables comparison with Christianity (2); prevents the accusation Christianity is being thrust down the pupil's throat (1); widening experience for later judgment (1); shows up the arrogance of old-fashioned European Christianity (1); as a supplement to normal studies (2); helps in search for common religious denominator (1).

b. When the figures are broken down in this fashion the numbers are so small that they cannot be used as the basis for any theory. The sole reason for their inclusion is to illustrate the spread of values noted by 'Leavers' as compared with 'Expansionists'. To compare attitudes more precisely a much larger survey is called for.

TABLE 10. Analysis of Table 8

Question: *What disadvantages and/or dangers might arise, in your opinion, from CSR in schools?*

	Expansionists	Leavers
None	18	5
Danger of over-simplification	5	3
Detract from teaching of Christianity	5	10
Too difficult and likely to cause confusion	4	11
Likely to be badly taught	2	4

Note: a. Other disadvantages noted, all by 'Leavers': boring (2); may emphasize racial differences (2); skirts the real issues (1); more important alternatives (2); no point in teaching CSR (1).

b. It should be noted that the totals in this Table are lower than in Table 8 since the views of the small sub-groups (Table 9) have been omitted.

Another teacher wrote that he could see no educational problems if the material was handled 'competently *and* sympathetically'.

It is interesting to note that of all the theoretical problems or objections raised 59% of them were raised by RE specialists, and only 41% by head-teachers (see Table 8). These figures cannot be dismissed simply on the grounds that head-teachers rushed their answers and gave less thought to the problems, since their answers to the questions on the values of CSR and whether it should be an examination subject were carefully answered.

Turning to practical difficulties, the lack of suitable teaching materials was noted more by RE specialists than by head-teachers (Table 11). One teacher commented on the need for a cheap (*ca.* 6s.) sourcebook, and another on the poor standard of filmstrips, in particular on the number of external views of temples which soon become boring. Another criticized the books for dealing with the philosophies of the different religions rather than the general pattern of every day life of their adherents. These criticisms can be summed up in the words of a teacher who wrote:

The main difficulty is that there are no books which present the background, history, characters and ideals of the different religions (with illustrations) in a way comparable to that in which Christianity is presented.

A few expressed doubts about staffing problems. One head-teacher, for example, wrote: 'I guess that good teachers of the subject will be rare.'

Interestingly, only one person, and he a teacher, commented on the possible financial problems.

If the questionnaires are divided into 'Expansionists' and 'Leavers' again,[5] it is the 'Expansionists' who are aware of the

---

[5] The numbers of those who taught the subject in depth, or were opposed to the subject in the syllabus at all, were too small (6 in each case) to be incorporated into the body of the text as distinct groups. On the other hand they do represent the opposite ends of the spectrum and their views may be usefully summarized here. Those taking the subject in depth stressed the

practical problems involved in the subject. 61% of the 'Leavers' saw no practical problems as compared with only 23% of the 'Expansionists' (Table 12). Similarly the 'Leavers' were either completely unaware of the shortage of material, or knew of some that the others did not. The objection to CSR in schools, therefore, does not appear to be on practical grounds, but on ideological, or as noted above, on apologetic, grounds.

This conclusion is reinforced if one compares the attitudes of the two groups to CSR as an examination subject. The 'Leavers' are not as keen on CSR forming an examination subject as are the 'Expansionists', yet the majority of them still view it as such (Table 13). Further, there is little difference between the two groups on the question of the suitability of the material for the whole secondary school age range (Table 14). This implies that they do not oppose the subject on the grounds that the material is necessarily too complex or difficult, so that we are thrown back to the original suggestion that the objection is largely on apologetic grounds.

The overall conclusions derived from this survey may be summarized under six points.

1. The subject is widely taught in schools in the West Riding, probably more widely than is generally realized, and usually as part of RE. In view of the extent to which it is taught, and the desire for its expansion it is a great pity that the subject is not given more attention in educational syllabuses. In the West Riding syllabus, for example, which is 132 pages long, only

---

value of the subject in promoting an awareness of man, rather than the relevance to the immigrant problem (although this was noted), or deepening the pupil's understanding of Christianity. They encountered few practical difficulties other than the shortage of suitable books, and the main educational problem they believed to be the danger of superficiality. It was their opinion that the subject was suitable for the whole secondary school age range, and generally favoured its inclusion as an examination subject. Those who opposed the introduction of the subject in any form were agreed in their judgment that the subject had little or no value. They believed that it would cause confusion in the pupil's mind and felt that it would detract from Christianity. On the practical side, they thought there was neither time, suitable staff or books to enable the subject to be introduced.

TABLE 11. Practical problems involved in CSR.
Question: *What are the practical problems involved in the teaching of CSR in schools?*

	Head-teachers	RE Specialists
None	13	12
Shortage of suitable books	7	14
Shortage of trained staff	7	5
Lack of time	4	10
Parental or Social objections	3	2
Problems with mixed ability groups	1	5
Finances	0	1

Note: Some respondents noted more than one problem, hence the total exceeds the number of respondents.

TABLE 12. Analysis of Table 11
Question: *What are the practical problems, in your opinion, involved in the teaching of CSR in schools?*

	Expansionists	Leavers
Shortage of suitable books	16	2
Lack of time	9	4
None	7	17
Shortage of trained staff	5	3
Parental or Social objections	3	1
Problems with mixed-ability groups	3	3
Finance	1	0

Note: It should be noted that the totals are often lower than in Table 11 since the views of the small sub-groups have been omitted.

TABLE 13. Analysis of Table 7
Question: *What are your feelings about CSR forming all or part of a paper in an external examination (CSE, GCE 'O' or 'A' level)?*

	Expansionists	Leavers	Totals
Yes, in some form	26	17	43
Not at all	5	11	16

Note: It should be noted that the totals are lower than in Table 7 since the views of the small sub-groups have been omitted.

TABLE 14. Analysis of Table 6
Question on the suitability of material for the different age groups.

	Expansionists	Leavers	Totals
CSR is a subject suitable for the whole school	19	17	36
14-18 age group only	8	5	13
16-18 age group only	2	4	6
Categories not accepted	2	2	4

Note: It should be noted that the totals are lower than in Table 6 since the views of the small sub-groups have been omitted.

three-quarters of a page is devoted to CSR.

2. There is overwhelming support for the continued existence of the subject in the syllabus, and a considerable demand for its expansion. Any movement to effect this expansion, however, must take into account the objections to the subject which appear to be based mainly on apologetic grounds. One may infer from this that were CSR to be accepted by education authorities as a fully contributing part of the total syllabus, a considerable education programme would be required to present CSR to some of the teachers themselves.

3. CSR is thought by a large majority to be a suitable subject for all age groups in the secondary school. This must be taken into account in the preparation of suitable teaching material.

4. An even larger majority than that mentioned in 3 would like to see the subject incorporated into the examination system. It is to be hoped, therefore, that more Boards will give this matter their serious consideration. On the other hand it would be interesting to know how many teachers make use of the provisions that already exist, e.g., CSE Mode III.

5. The chief practical difficulties facing the subject are lack of books, suitable teaching aids, time and staff. In view of the demand that has been seen to exist the academic and educational worlds ought to consider their responsibility in the provision of materials and the appropriate training, so that the supply may soon match the demand.

6. Perhaps the most striking feature of the respondents answers was that the value of CSR was seen in a much wider context than the traditional RE lesson. Its values were seen to be primarily the increase in tolerance and understanding, the widening of the pupil's educational horizons, as well as deepening his understanding of man and the world. For those concerned with the expansion of CSR perhaps the question should be whether or not CSR should be thought of as a subject quite independent of the traditional RE lesson?

John R. Hinnells is Lecturer in Religious Studies, University of Newcastle upon Tyne.

A Humanist Approach to the Teaching of Religion in Schools

H. J. BLACKHAM

POLITICAL BACKGROUND

In the USA religion is kept out of the public schools by law on political grounds. In England and Wales religion is put into these schools by law on political grounds. In America the situation represents a stalemate in the sectarian battle for the mind of the child. Here it represents a compromise by which the Anglican Church kept a stake in education but gave up to the local education authorities a large number of parochial schools, on the guarantee that the school day would begin with a corporate act of worship and that religious instruction would be given on the basis of a syllabus locally agreed in which Anglicans would have a voice. Since 1944, RI and the act of worship have been politically imposed on the county schools in this way, but those who have been trained to give effect to the religious clauses of the Act have over the years come to take a strictly educational view of their task: RI has by common consent become RE. 'Indoctrination' is a dirty word, and any intention of evangelization in the schools has been disavowed explicitly and authoritatively.

However, there has been some double-think and some double-talk about this, with statements, in particular from the Anglican Church, that would seem to see in the county schools the key sector in any strategy for the re-conversion of England. Certainly, politicians fear that the churches will fight to retain compulsion and that they can rely on the backing of public opinion: and for this reason no politician will touch the question unless and until forced to by an evident change in public opinion. Those who have been active in defence of compulsion, have cited opinion polls which show an overwhelming majority of parents and of teachers in favour of keeping the rules as they are. Humanists have been critical of these polls not only on technical grounds but also because the questions asked could not provide a reliable guide to what parents really want for their children. Therefore the British Humanist Association commissioned National Opinion Polls Limited to carry out a survey in March 1969. 1,905 electors drawn from the electoral list were interviewed, and asked to choose from a list of eight purposes of education what they thought most important, next most important, and least important in the education of schoolboys and of schoolgirls over 12. They were also asked which of a list of six items were legally required in state schools. This last question revealed widespread ignorance of what is legally required. For both boys and girls, the highest number of first and second choices were 'Training for a career' and 'Help in becoming an adult with a sense of right and wrong'. The religious purposes of education ('Help in becoming a convinced Christian'; 'Information about Christianity and other world religions') received comparatively low ratings. Break-downs were given for sex, age, social class, religion, political party, and region.[1] A further survey is being commissioned by the British Humanist Association, but the purpose is mainly to counter the rash use that has been made of previous polls. No serious argument for the construction of public policy should be built on the narrow and shallow foundation of such procedures.

Of course, education cannot be kept out of politics. The funds are allocated in competition with other claims. The Soviet Sputnik changed the government's attitude overnight, and gave education a priority it had previously lacked. The only way for educational interests to prevail is for educators to stand together for what they think is educationally right and to make

---

[1] The report available from BHA, 13 Prince of Wales Terrace, London W.8, price 5s.

their informed opinion known. Recent discussion of religious and moral education has shown that an enlightened body of opinion is being formed which does not hold with the 1944 rules; and there is evidence that this opinion is having influence with the education authorities.

MORAL EDUCATION

Part of the function of RE was assumed to be moral education, but recently an independent approach to moral education is being explored and developed. The most conspicuous example is the project of the Farmington Trust Research Unit at Oxford whose director, John Wilson, has explained its guiding principles in a book.[2] By its side, in Oxford, is the Schools Council's Moral Education Curriculum Project. The new lectureships in the philosophy of education in the colleges of education are also concerned with this development.

This new approach is abundantly justified for the following reasons.

1. Morality has always had its own ground as an inescapable requirement of any society. This independence has been studied sociologically, and recognized academically in philosophical ethics for centuries.

2. A distinction is necessary between a public realm of obligation, in which one is bound by the social rules for living and working together, and a private realm of choice, in which one is free to follow one's own beliefs and ideals, which may be a religious faith. The public realm includes the school community, from which there can be no opting out; it is here that the foundations and binding character of moral obligation are experienced as well as understood.

3. If morality is taught as part of Christianity, there is a danger that those who reject the beliefs when they leave school are likely to discard the morals as well. There are different views about the relations of Christianity and morals, which need not affect an independent approach. Christians will bring to morality

[2] An Introduction to Moral Education, John Wilson et al., Pelican, London, 1968.

their own motives, insights, resources, sanctions; what these are is part of the teaching of what Christianity is. This depends on belief, and does not displace rational consideration for the interests of others and rational criticism and justification of behaviour.

4. Most important, moral education cannot be left to RE and the RE specialist because it is the concern of the whole school. The head, the staff, the pupils, all have their necessary parts in moral education, whatever their personal convictions. Basically, moral education is the way the school is organized and run.

RELIGIOUS EDUCATION

How is Christianity to be taught, if it is to be education and not indoctrination? Sometimes it is said that it should be teaching 'about' the faith, not teaching the faith; or teaching 'how', not teaching 'that'. I would describe the proper object of the teaching as an understanding of Christianity, its origins, its historical influence and what it means to believers in their personal lives. All this is factual, even when it is 'bearing witness'. Beyond this, the study of Christianity is a study of the kind of thing religion is, its distinction from, or its affinity to science and the arts and other types of experience. In all these ways, the subject can be on the same footing as other subjects—open to investigation and discussion.

There are two main difficulties from a Humanist point of view: the corporate act of worship, and what is to be done in the primary school. The act of worship enjoined on the school as a whole by the 1944 Act assumes that the school is a Christian community. The school is thus brought together either as an incomplete community or as an insincere one; and since the school community is the foundation of moral education this is a bad start, not only to the school day but also to all that goes on in the name of moral education. Granted that worship is the central Christian experience, and that Christian education should provide an opportunity for participation in this experience, it should be conducted by believers for believers, with an open invitation to all to attend. However, RE is not Christian education quite in this sense. If it were, the study of Buddhism should include practise in meditation or other such techniques, since, in terms of an educational approach, it is on the same footing as the study of Christianity. In sum, worship as an extra-curricular activity should be open to all, but not as a corporate act of the school as a mixed community or as a community purged by abstentions.

The difficulty in the primary school is both in the integrated curriculum, which makes nonsense of excusal, and in the immaturity of the pupil, so that there can hardly be the examination and discussion of experience which become possible in the secondary school. The Plowden Report mentioned all the difficulties, and ignored them. The Report insisted that children should not be disturbed by controversy, that they should be taught the faith about which they can make up their own minds later. Undoubtedly, the temptation not to indoctrinate but to induct young children into religious faith is very strong. Plowden blesses the attempt; another document speaks of the Christian faith as an 'assimilated assumption' when the child comes to the secondary school. Humanists object to this very strongly: it is not education; it is not fair to the child that is not from a Christian home; it is a different approach from that thought proper in the secondary school, and no proper justification of the difference has been offered: there is no need from a Christian point of view for this difference. Accepting the Piaget-Goldman findings about the unfortunate effects of attempts at conceptual teaching at this stage of education, there are two things that can be done which ought to be acceptable to both Christians and Humanists. Children of this age are natural anthropologists and are interested in differences in ways of life in the world about them. This is the time at which to make them acquainted with the facts of religious differences in the community as concretely as possible, since it is part of their education, and at this stage imposes no strain on them for they are not required to make decisions. Secondly, the fundamental experiences of being loved and cared for, of sharing, of sympathy with the suffering of others, of forgiving and being

forgiven, are more important at this stage than is the
interpretation. On these lines, by attending to format.
ences and postponing questions of their interpretation
ties in the primary school of reconciling a Christia
Humanist approach, otherwise insuperable, can be av

THE COMPARATIVE STUDY OF RELIGION

Humanists have long favoured the study of world religions in
school, and should welcome a new movement to promote it.
Their main objection to the teaching of Christianity has been
its exclusiveness. For myself, I have been sceptical about this as
practicable because it seemed to me that 'comparative religion'
was an advanced study beyond the scope of the school and remote in interest, there were not enough competent teachers
available, and not likely to be, and the curriculum was already
overburdened. I am revising this opinion in the light of the new
interest there is in the subject and an evident intention to try
to meet the difficulties. If there is a widespread will to take and
tackle the subject seriously, the difficulties melt away and are
replaced by considerable advantages. I would underline three of
them, from a Humanist point of view.

First, education is broadened by including some acquaintance
with the diversity of cultures in the world. Learning how others
live, think, feel is education, on its humanistic side. To exclude
all cultures but our own would seem primitive, a refusal of
education, if we were not so used to it. Immigrant groups in our
own society and the shrinkage of the world by rapid communications have made this particularism look as parochial as it is. The
danger of prejudice in race relations has flared up as one of the
major menaces to world order. For all these reasons, acceptance
of the study of world religions in the schools on a footing of
equality would be a turning-point in education of major importance in principle.

Second, education would not only be broadened but also
deepened. Standards are formed only by comparisons. Within
any one culture no fundamental comparison that brings under
examination basic assumptions is possible. Hindu presupposi-

tions and concepts differ profoundly from those that have been formed under Christian influence. Christian concepts, and many that are current in secular society, cannot be appreciated nor criticized nor firmly held until they are seen in the light of alternatives. The distinctive attitude to life in Western culture is not distinctively human. How far each way of being human is cultural, not universal, is appreciated only in comparative studies. The claims of each religion or culture are not thereby debunked. They may be given a more realistic assessment and a more tenable interpretation.

Third, a study of religions other than Christianity as well as of Christianity is an opportunity for the study of religion as such, as a distinctive type of experience. The religious categories (divine, holy, sacred, numinous, eternal, Being, absolute, ultimate reality) are all by definition other than human. What do they correspond to in human experience? Or what is there in human experience that brought about their invention? Comparison of world religions is a method of exploring these categories within their own terms, rather than by contrast with non-religious or purely human categories. But they can be studied also in other contexts, such as that provided by William James[3] and more recently by Marghanita Laski.[4] Within Western cultural tradition, there is in Platonism and in Stoicism and in some pre-Socratics an affinity with the metaphysical thinking characteristic of the East.

This study of religion on the sides of metaphysics and psychology should be supplemented by a study of the sociological aspect. This includes attention to the dark side of the historical record of religions—persecutions, exterminations, wars. The Old Testament provides materials, and so does Church history. Moralization of the concept of God in the O.T. and the eventual establishment of religious freedom and toleration in Europe and America exemplify development and progress in religion as in other human affairs, with the inference that this still goes on.

[3] *Varieties of Religious Experience*, William James, Fontana, London, 1960.
[4] *Ecstasy*, A Study of some Secular and Religious Experiences, Marghanita Laski, Cresset Press, London, 1961.

The history also exemplifies the inertia of institutions and their tendency to corrupt, which makes perpetual the need for renewal and reform. As Reinhold Niebuhr once remarked: 'The Church may be Anti-Christ; and if it does not think so, it is.'

This disciplined study of other faiths, that might include non-religious faiths, such as Marxism and Humanism, would not be to provide live options for the choice of boys and girls at school, a faith to live by to take away with them. That would not be realistic, and is not the function of education. Rather, it would be an attempt to give some insight into different ways of thinking about the world and human life, some sense of the history of ideas, some understanding of distinctively religious experience and claims. These are beginnings, the opening of doors, the looking at maps; not actual explorations. But this is all that education at school in other subjects can hope to do. To enlarge the sample of what there is in the world of interest and use that can be offered at school enlarges opportunity, and is of untold benefit to many.

A NEW DESIGN

There are now these three independent programmes established or starting: RE under the 1944 rules; moral education; the study of world religions. Together, these form a broad general area of inter-related studies. Under what direction are they to be co-ordinated and developed? Clearly, the 1944 rules are out-of-date, and no longer relate to the actualities of the situation nor serve the educational needs of the present generation in this field. Repeal of the compulsory clauses of the Act would not bring religious education to an end in any school, but would allow flexibility in the arrangements made for it. The colleges and institutes of education and the interested voluntary associations are quite capable of providing the stimulus, information, materials, methods, and techniques required for teaching in this field and for the production of syllabuses and programmes, without the political procedures which enabled the churches to have a finger in the pie. The educational interests will be taken care of without compulsion, and other interests have been disavowed.

The mere removal of compulsion would not create order where there is already a great deal of diversity, if not confusion. Uniformity is not desirable, but everywhere the three interests should be served. Whatever is done in any county school should be educational in good faith, providing no excuse to anyone for opting out. And the programmes should be such that staff of different personal convictions can co-operate in them. With these general principles, religious and moral education should be left in the hands of educators. There are no necessary conflicts in serving the interests of RE, moral education, and the study of world religions. They can and should supplement one another. To insist on including them all under RE and the 1944 rules is almost unthinkable at this time of day. If there are barricades to be manned, they are put up against any remnant of the old guard that would attack the new positions from that quarter. Young people should learn the nature, conditions and obligations of morality, should be put on the road to responsible choice of the beliefs and ideals by which they will live, and should be shown how to look to horizons beyond the culture in which they are bred and the conclusions to which they will come. I know of no reason why Christians and Humanists cannot agree about this, and I have reason to think there is none.

H. J. Blackham was the first Director of the British Humanist Association.

A Christian Approach to the Comparative Study of Religion in Schools

O. R. JOHNSTON

The title of this paper is one which needs particular attention, and I must first define my terms of reference. I am concerned with *a* Christian approach rather than *the* Christian approach. I shall approach the subject from a specifically confessional standpoint, though there is by no means complete agreement amongst those who claim the name of Christian about the study of world religions and it is quite possible for other Christians to adopt different approaches without logical inconsistency. I speak for nobody but myself.

But in what sense am I using the term 'Christian'? To which believing tradition do I belong? It is better to be explicit about this at the start too, so that readers are not set off on a detective trail or a witch-hunt at later stages. My own Christian approach is that of an Anglican—one whose church is catholic (inheriting much of its external structure and its creeds from the church of earlier centuries), reformed (in that it accepts the constant need to stand under the authority of the apostolic witness of Scripture, hence the break with Rome at the Reformation) and established (living a life intertwined by scores of subtle links, some institutionalized, some not, with the life of the English nation). Along the liberal-conservative spectrum of theological opinion, which is fully represented at all points within the Church of England, I would place myself at the conservative end. Though this is my 'convictional' position, I am not suggesting that others have no right to claim the name of Christian unless they share my views; I am merely making clear my own religious allegiance,

59

and how I shall tend to use the word 'Christian'.

It is, I hope, likely that many who would not share my religious conviction could nevertheless share at least some of my conclusions about the place of CSR in schools, or even—at the very least—find some interest in seeing how someone so tainted with reactionary Christian orthodoxy looks at world religions!

'Schools' is in fact the next word in my title, and I should like to stress here that I am trying to explore the best approach to this subject for the schools of *this* country, England in the twentieth century. Schools are not disembodied, they cannot exist in a vacuum. Rather are they part of a particular society with a particular cultural inheritance. There is a danger that those who do not discern the various educational issues involved in asking or expecting the schools to do any particular thing will fail to appreciate the complex philosophical, religious and sociological background of our enquiry. The school situation itself comprises a vast bundle of expectations—those of the parents, of the children taught, of the wider community in its various aspects, academic, commercial, political and so on. If the prospect of CSR in schools tempts us to move forward with all speed, it is worth while reminding ourselves that we do not prescribe *de novo*. We do not have enough knowledge (Loukes and Alves notwithstanding)[1] to be able to say whether 'traditional school RI'—if it exists!—is either so bad that it must cease, or that it is so good that it must clearly be retained.

When we come to the term 'religion' we embark upon the main body of this paper. Professor Hilliard's article deals most adequately with the position of the subject in the schools, and I conceive it to be my task to look rather at religion in general from a Christian point of view. Here again definition is all-important.

Religion is an ever-recurring phenomenon in human history, but it is difficult if not impossible to characterize in essence. It springs from vision, demands commitment and gives direction to human life. Men will say, 'I am not what I was before I *saw* . . .', 'I was a different man before I *trusted* . . .', 'Now

[1] See Bibliography, p. 110.

I have begun my pilgrimage . . .'. Perhaps we can get no nearer than that. As an object of study, however, religion may be fairly characterized as a multi-dimensional phenomenon. Professor Smart charts this most subtly and suggestively in his *Secular Education and the Logic of Religion*,[2] examining the various aspects he isolates. These are the dimensions he names: doctrinal, mythological (the stories), ethical, ritual, experiential and social or institutional. I suspect we shall find this analysis extraordinarily influential and fruitful in the future study of CSR.

The history of civilization shows how religion has provided the mainspring of some of the noblest—and the basest—of human achievements. It has entered the whole texture of life in every culture known to us. It has provided a means of social control of unparalleled effectiveness. It has given coherence, purpose and joy to the lives of countless thousands since the dawn of history. For this reason it is clearly a dimension of human experience and aspiration which cannot be dismissed in any estimate of man, nor in any comparison of differing estimates, nor in any search for truth about man and his universe and hence in any educational programme worth the name. All this may be said with fair assurance without accepting the postulates of any one religion, or indeed of any religion at all.

The roots of a consistent Christian approach to the study of religion must lie in the understanding of God's relation to man and the world. This understanding is formulated in the doctrines of creation and redemption, and hence the first part of this paper must necessarily deal with these doctrines. When he studies religion, the Christian finds a certain tension between the doctrine of creation and the doctrine of redemption.

Christianity has always asserted strongly that this is God's world. The church has always rejected as un-Christian any ultimate dualism. 'Jehovah reigns' would not be an inadequate way to describe the message of either the first or the last chapters of the Bible. The Christian doctrine of Creation is far more than the weak deism which sees God as the celestial designer and engineer who planned and made all things (though it does

[2] Chapter 1. See Bibliography, p. 111.

assert that too). Rather does it depict God as the Governor of all things and all events at all times, the great Sustainer who 'upholds all things by the word of his power' (Heb. 1:3). History is a great canvas He is painting; individuals are persons in a story He is telling. In consequence, human history and culture cannot, for the Christian, be a fortuitous progression of events, a 'tale told by an idiot signifying nothing'. There is a broad frame of significance to life and to all human achievement, though we may not always discern it. The Christian doctrine of providence, which springs from the view of God as Creator, is not without its difficulties, of course. But it has certain emphases which delineate the Christian view of the world.

If we look at the mythical structure given in the early chapters of Genesis, we find the characteristic themes of this Christian frame of significance—man as made in God's image, a personal, rational moral being, man as God's vice-regent, put in charge of the natural order to 'have dominion over it and subdue it', and man as a social being, differentiated by divine purpose into two sexes, commanded to multiply, and bound by the deepest and subtlest human bond, the gift of language. From this picture two conclusions are usually drawn: first, that a relation with God is built into human existence and hence a transcendent reference will constantly and inevitably crop up throughout human experience, and second, the fact that as man reflects on himself and his world, mapping out his own mental and emotional development and the story of his whole cultural progress, this religious factor will emerge as a legitimate field of study.

The second group of assertions which the Christian makes are those concerned with the Christian doctrine of redemption. Genesis proceeds to its third chapter, telling of 'man's first disobedience', and the story of the Bible becomes a history of restoration and healing, *Heilsgeschichte* as the German theologians have it. While there is no space to enter into the full implications of this, it must be pointed out here that religion changes its character as a result of human sin. What might have been untrammelled communion with the divine became for the whole race a search, a quest with many a wrong turning. Hostility and guilt became an inseparable element in the religious consciousness. The relationship between God and man became a love-hate relationship, a complex and uncomfortable thing; God was holy, completely 'other'. And because guilt must be purged and hostility reconciled the almost universal practice of sacrifice emerges, underscoring (for the Christian) the need for a way of approach and reconciliation. The nature of the Divine Being becomes obscured, and men fumble their way into idolatry more often than not, as Paul describes so graphically in the first chapter of his Letter to the Romans.

From the standpoint of the doctrines of sin and salvation then, religions will tend to be buildings erected on the shaky basis of a dim consciousness of the transcendent which is built into human nature, but constructed of constantly distorted materials, insights twisted by human selfishness and rebellion. Since man lost his first unsullied vision of his Maker he has been religiously at sea, and hence the conflicting and manifold expressions of 'religion'—animism, polytheisn, pantheism and even atheism.

But this is by no means the end of the story. The Christian goes on to assert that man's faulty vision is corrected by revelation, God shows himself first to the nation of Israel and then comes personally in Jesus Christ. Hence the Bible and hence the Christian message with its pregnant title 'good news'. This gospel announces clarity in place of obscurity, republishing the nature of the one almighty Creator and Sustainer of all things. It is noteworthy that the apostolic preaching recorded in the Book of Acts is concerned with *reminding* men rather than announcing something brand new. Men should have been and were in fact 'feeling after God' as Paul put it at Athens (Acts 17:27). But the knowledge they had hitherto possessed—outside Israel at any rate—was fragmentary and distorted. In and through Jesus Christ, what Israel had been told clearly but failed to absorb, to treasure and to spread to the nations was unmistakably declared by the presence of God in His Son with new and dazzling clarity. And by this same event—the coming of the Son of God —reconciliation was effected. By His death and resurrection, the early preachers announced, Jesus of Nazareth had overcome death and dealt with all the transgressions of a new people of God, a restored humanity. The offer of free unmerited reconciliation must now be proclaimed to all men because all men needed it. The conviction of the supremacy, the finality and the complete adequacy of the new 'religion' was what made the church a missionary church, a remarkable religious phenomenon by any standards, whatever may be one's judgment of its theology. As I see the Christian's position then, if he speaks *qua* Christian, from within his own tradition of belief, Christianity is the religion to end all religions. It implies a judgment upon all other religious systems, ancient or modern. Truth, finality and clarity are given in Christ.

But we must add that this does *not* imply that there is no value in the study of other religions. From the formal point of view, Christianity is an observable human phenomenon, it remains *a* religion. Commitment, as Professor Smart has emphasized, is not necessarily a hindrance to the study of religions. For if a Christian takes the doctrines of Creation and Providence seriously, he is bound to see religion as a part of God's world and a field of human endeavour and exploration. There are analogies from other fields of human knowledge here. A Christian will, for example, attach a particular significance to the physical world around him, it is God's creation—yet he can be an honest and competent natural scientist. Similarly a Christian views the human body with respect and wonder as in many ways the final masterpiece of God's handiwork, but there is nothing to prevent his becoming a skilled physiologist, anatomist or pathologist. A Christian will attach special significance to certain historical events which took place nineteen and a half centuries ago in the Near East, but this does not prevent his becoming a competent historian of that or any other period. In just this same way a Christian attaches a specific value to one particular religion, yet there is nothing which need prevent his becoming a student of one or more of the other religions. It is perfectly possible for a Christian to welcome and advocate the study of world religions if he holds a proper doctrine of creation in tension with his equally important doctrine of redemption.

But we may go further than this. A Christian studying world religions may well find his studies fruitful and advantageous even from the standpoint of his own faith. He may find, firstly, that his deepening acquaintance with other religions draws attention to forgotten or neglected elements in his own religious tradition. From its history we can see that the Christian church has by no means been free of distortions, over-simplifications and exaggerations. In western Protestant countries there has been, since the Reformation, a constant tendency to activism. At its best this has exemplified the all-embracing nature of Christian concern for humanity, the dynamic evangelistic outreach of the New Testament church and a powerful pressure for economic and social progress. But in some respects this activism has obscured the contemplative stress, the devotional element of personal communion with God which is clear in the New Testament, but which we have found easy to forget. The counsels of meditation which are to be found in so many of the world's other religions can draw attention to neglected elements in the church's own faith. Doubtless many other examples could be given by more learned students than myself.

The second possibility which I should like to adduce is a more sociological one. The study of world religions may underscore recurrent tendencies in the development of religious institutions within Christendom. I believe that CSR can provide the Christian with a most valuable socio-historical perspective. To take but one example again (and at the risk of great oversimplification) can it not be said that the rise of priestcraft within Christianity becomes better understood when one sees it as another example of a much wider religious phenomenon? One interesting theory maintains that the rise of priestcraft in other world religions is intimately connected with urban development and the differentiation of economic and political functions which accompanied the rise of the city-state. City life and the emergence of more clearly defined social functions provokes a certain sophistication, and an attitude of contempt for earlier and simpler forms of religious expression connected with the pastoral or patriarchal society. The right to sacrifice becomes vested, for example, in certain cultic experts. The rise of priest-craft within Christendom may have an interesting parallel in what happened in India in the second millennium B.C., when a priestly caste emerged with the invasion of the Indo-Iranians. Protestants at least will label this as 'degeneration' and find the other examples of the process most illuminating.

Thirdly, I would suggest that the comparative study of religions may well help us to a better appreciation of certain problem areas within our own religious tradition. Christian mysticism has always seemed to many to be a sort of erratic block in our religious tradition. Many Christians have been hesitant to estimate its significance and to evaluate its function. I should not be surprised if cross-cultural religious studies in the field of religious awareness, the psychological or experiential dimension of CSR, were to provide great help here.

Fourthly, the study of world religions surely fosters cultural understanding. The Christian has no stakes in cultural isolation-ism. He believes in good neighbourliness on a national as well as on a personal level. We must understand the problems of India, Pakistan or Burma better if we are to offer them the help and sympathy they need. Similarly with the various ethnic groups in our own land; this is the whole thrust of Dr Par-rinder's contribution. CSR cannot fail to help us to a deeper understanding of our neighbours, and no Christian, whatever his attitude to the problems of immigration, would want to deny the need for such understanding.

Finally—and perhaps a little more speculatively—it seems to me not unlikely that many young people who rejected Chris-tianity (or what they conceived to be Christianity) at an early age due, perhaps, to parental apathy or to the sneering hostility of their adolescent peer-group, might well be encouraged to give it new and more sympathetic consideration after a look at the various other world religions. I should not rate this high on my list of reasons for encouraging the study of religions, but it seems to me to be quite probable that not a few students might well come back to take a more sympathetic and less jaundiced view of the historic faith of western Europe if their understanding could be stimulated by examining the various ways of the East.

But if there are good reasons for supposing that Christians ought to welcome the study of world religions, there are also reasons why the Christian student of religions—the intelligent, thoughtful, open Christian student, that is—has something of real value to offer to the discipline of CSR itself.

First, he can offer a consciousness of the religious dimension of human experience. Admittedly some religions do not go as far as Christianity in its assertion that God is personal and the soul of man, personal and indestructible. Yet it seems to me that all religions do try to point to a dimension beyond that of immediate sense-experience of the physical world, to a transcendent realm of some sort which gives ultimate significance to the material here-and-now. To begin, as any Christian would, with this as part of one's own personal religious equipment is surely a help to any student of religion, though of course it brings a certain risk as well. There will be the danger of too facile an equivalence being postulated between Christian and other religious concepts and experiences. Superficial similarities can be deceptive. Yet a fundamental sympathy remains, and is surely a help to the understanding of religious phenomena.

Secondly, a Christian may well be able to supply considerable skill in the use of religious concepts. Granted, not all concepts are common to all religions; some only occur in one or two. I am sure a vast amount of map work in comparative logical geography remains to be done. When one thinks of holiness, eternity, salvation, bliss, torment, judgment, reward, sacrifice, soul . . . the immensity and complexity of the task is almost overwhelming. The linguistic and conceptual problems here will be very great. But I am sure that this task must be attempted; indeed I would say that we *must* achieve some measure of real and agreed success here before we send teachers scurrying back to their classrooms to embark on world religions with the third forms. We cannot hope to do anything of real intellectual integrity in our schools if we have not provided the teachers at

least (some would say the pupils as well) with reliable reference
books on areas of overlap and difference between the religious
concepts of Christianity on the one hand and any other religion
we may wish youngsters to study on the other. If we do not
produce such works, we shall be encouraging facile equivalences
and superficial antitheses in children's thinking about world
religions. But to return to the main point here—Christians have
behind them several centuries of theological tradition during
which certain terms and concepts have been refined and clarified.
This work has continued to our own day (one need only mention the names of Ian Ramsey, now Bishop of Durham, and of
Professor Smart) and a Christian who is conscious of these dis-
cussions, past and present, will be well equipped in the field
of the study of world religions.

Thirdly—and perhaps paradoxically—the Christian student
can bring to this field a clarity of vision born of Christian confidence. This is by no means easy to express. Perhaps we may
approach it in this way: Christians would not be Christians if
they did not assert something unique about Jesus Christ. He
said: 'I am the truth', and His followers called Him 'God mani-
fest in the flesh.' They spoke of Christians as those who 'obey
the truth' or believe 'the word of truth'. At its best therefore
(an important qualification!) Christian faith engenders not only
confidence in Jesus Christ as God and Saviour but also a robust
desire to enter into dialogue with all men with a sharpened
awareness of the difference between truth and falsehood. The
Christian who is worth his salt has a constant desire to defend,
to explain, to expound and to apply his faith to all men and in
all situations, just because he is convinced that it is so adequate
for all needs. He has something of supreme value to share. He
wants to convince and to convert those who are opposed. His
model here is the Apostle Paul at Ephesus, who was willing to
argue and debate with all comers (Acts 19:8-9). Nor does this
inhibit wider sympathy.

Strangely enough such conviction need not militate against
a frank and fair appreciation of the great religions; rather does it
sharpen the Christian's desire to know just what the other

religion is really saying, what its adherents are concerned to assert and how their beliefs cohere in a total picture of the world, what sort of life they lead in consequence, what sort of society they desire, and whether their faith is personally satisfying. It is interesting to note here that a man with such a definite Christian commitment as Professor Zaehner is an authority on Hinduism. Similarly one of our leading experts on the faith of Islam (Professor Norman Anderson) is a conservative evangelical Christian in the Church of England. One must freely admit that there are obscurantists—some fearful, others stubborn—in the Christian church. But my own belief is that if Christian faith can only be held at the expense of a *sacrificium intellectu*, an ostrich-like ignorance of other cultures and other belief-systems, then such a brand of Christian faith is scarcely worth having. Certainly it would seem to surrender the New Testament claim of Christianity to be 'the truth' in any real sense. I am convinced that the way of dialogue and exploration is more genuinely achieved on the basis of an intelligent faith in the way I have indicated above, and I believe this to be more truly a Christian position. All these things I see as distinctive and extremely valuable contributions which Christians can make, and I am sure are already making, to the comparative study of religions.

Finally, I wish to comment briefly on the school situation. Here I am in complete agreement with all that Professor Hilliard was written. Basically, as I have tried to show above, there are no reasons why Christians should stay out of study in this field. But the school situation does present vast problems. Even assuming that there is interest and enthusiasm, to be able to transmit anything like an adequate understanding of another religion is a truly Herculean task. Stories must be told, a moral framework (often quite remote from anything the child has ever experienced) must be grasped or felt, a strange way of worship must somehow be apprehended and an alien social structure understood. All these form the various dimensions of what it *means* to be an adherent of another religion. We have a whole new culture-picture to build up in a child's mind, and we cannot always call on our immigrants, because many are rapidly becoming atypical of their ancestral faith, owing to cultural assimilation in Britain.

Given the right conditions and the right resources, the job could be done. But I think it not very likely that it can ever be done successfully on a very large scale, and then only with well-motivated teenage students. We should need time in school which not even RE of the more usual type can get at present, though perhaps with integrated studies and team-teaching it may be possible to undertake more thorough concentrated projects, e.g. three weeks' work on India, full-time. If we can get the time, we shall then need the materials, above all colour films to bring to life the land, the people and the worship. This I believe to be the only real way to see religion in its proper context—as a whole way of life. I believe that even the cameraman who makes the film should be a Hindu for our Indian films —how much can be suggested by a camera angle or a detailed close-up of a face or a statue! And we would need teaching of a very high order, the teachers supplied with reference material to enable them to understand at a deeper adult level the internal structure of belief and the dominant modes of feeling characteristic of the religion that is being explored. Given the time, the resources and the teachers, then, something may be attempted. But let us not underestimate the complexity and difficulty of the task if we are to set our hands to CSR in schools.

I hope that I have shown that in principle I see no objection to the Christian studying or teaching world religion. But now that we have descended to the school situation, the final question which might well be asked is: Where does this leave traditional 'Christian' school RE? My answer would be: It leaves it just where it is, but enriched by fruitful dialogue with another world religion where we are fortunate enough to be able to do this *properly*. But looking at religious education generally, it is clearly the first aim of the nation's schools to initiate children into the cultural heritage of their own land, which in our case must involve a basic knowledge of the Christian faith. This is essential, and there are signs that we are now beginning to agree that this can be done in a genuinely 'open' manner and without the constant cry of 'indoctrination!'. Given broader and better teacher training, better resources of materials and time, the study of world religions will gradually and, I believe, rightly find its way into the work of the upper forms of secondary schools. No Christian need hesitate to help in this task for *religious* reasons, as I hope I have shown, though on educational grounds he might well be wary of trying to do too much too soon and finding that the last state is worse than the first.

O. R. Johnston is Lecturer in Education, University of Newcastle upon Tyne.

The Ethics and Customs of the Main Immigrant Peoples

E. G. PARRINDER

Migration is a regular feature of human life, but in recent years it has figured prominently in the news in this country. Great Britain has become a cosmopolitan country in a new way, as the result of an empire from which we enjoyed commercial fruits in past centuries. Now we are receiving much closer contact in our own land with the late imperial peoples than ever before. This is not to say that we have a backwash of inferior peoples, who can only be put to servile tasks in the South African manner and relegated to ghettos. On the contrary, there is a 'brain drain' from the late empire to this country, and our hospitals, transport, restaurants and many factories could not function without overseas workers.

Immigrants must be distinguished between visitors and more permanent workers. Among the temporary visitors are nearly all the Africans, the true negroes, who come to study in universities, technical colleges, and hospitals. Their languages, religions and customs are diverse, though the great majority who come here are Christian and have been educated in English. However they are rarely settlers and apart from hospital workers most of them return home fairly soon.

Similarly, students from European and Asian lands, with less knowledge of English, lighter and more varied colours, and different social customs, are only transitory passengers and few are true immigrants.

Statistics of Commonwealth immigrants fluctuate, do not compose the whole picture, and contain some surprises. In 1967 figures for immigrants into Britain were as follows:

Canada	121,000
Australia	82,000
New Zealand	24,000
India	57,000
Pakistan	44,000
Ceylon	5,000
West Indies	28,000
East Africa	7,000[1]

By far the largest numbers recorded therefore were white people from Canada and Australasia, but it is not necessary here to discuss the curious morals of the inhabitants of Kangaroo Valley or Montreal Place. Also there is no control over travel from Ireland and perhaps even greater numbers came from there, but there is no need for a discussion of the tribal customs of supporters of De Valera or Ian Paisley.

The problems of assimilating immigrant peoples centre principally round differences of colour and the variant customs of the new arrivals. It may be assumed that Canadians and Australians have much the same social and moral behaviour as ourselves, because they are largely of European descent. But West Indians may appear to be more difficult to assimilate, and Indians and Pakistanis even more so.

WEST INDIANS

The West Indian islands and tropical American mainland enclaves formerly under British colonial rule are places of mixed population. The great majority are descendants of African slaves, transported there by our forefathers from the sixteenth to the nineteenth centuries. There is a much smaller number of children, mostly mixed, of the ancient Caribs, but there are also important minorities of offspring of Indian and Chinese indentured labourers, taken there in the last century. There has been a great deal of racial mixture in the West Indies, not effected without tensions and leaving a legacy of snobbishness,

[1] Statistics from *Whittaker's Almanac*, 1969.

between white, brown and black populations. Many of those who are loosely called 'negro', in the Caribbean and America, are hardly distinguishable from some people of the Near or Middle East.

Social customs have been similarly modified. The effects of change upon Indian custom may be read in the sparkling novels of V. S. Naipaul, who himself shows the effect of English language and culture, not least in the shocks that he felt in a visit to India, described in *An Area of Darkness*. Some Asians have become Christian, and where they have not done so their Hindu and Muslim customs will be considered later.

Most of the West Indians are Christian. This is an important fact, both because of the close relationship that always exists between religion and morality, and because the common faith should ease integration into this officially Christian country. After early years of neglect, during which negro slaves were regarded as little better than animals, with no souls or religion, the Evangelical Revival brought missions which led them into Christianity. Their religion goes back several generations, and many of them have mothers and grandmothers who are Methodist or Baptist class-leaders and potent forces in family life. West Indians have often fitted into church life in England in a way that has rarely been possible for Indians and Pakistanis, though some have been cold-shouldered and others have founded their own churches.

The old African religions of the slaves had no scriptures and little widespread organization, and much of it was unable to survive deportation. Voodoo, however, a word derived from the Dahomean *vodun* for a 'god', contains some remains of old religious cults and a fair amount of magical practice. The magical side of Voodoo and Obeah (from the Ashanti *Obayifo* for a witch) developed under the disapproval of the official churches, but was helped on by romantic white participants. The social and ethical customs of old Africa have also largely disappeared; the food taboos belonging to religious cults were forgotten, the marriage rules were neglected or forcibly changed from without.

The language of the West Indian immigrants, like their official religion, is of British origin. They may be difficult to understand at times, though perhaps no more than a Cockney or an Aberdonian, and West Indian cricket commentators compare favourably in accent with Australians or South Africans. They are brought up in fully English schools, without even a vernacular such as true Africans have at Primary level. Their dress too is British. One of them laughed when his liberal English friends invited him to a fancy dress party and said, 'Come in your native dress.' He replied, 'Man, this is ma native dress.' Another startled a minister at a church door by asking, 'Can you get me a gun?' The minister thought the red revolution had begun and asked nervously what kind. He was reassured to get the reply, 'A gown like the one you are wearing. My brother is a minister too.'

West Indian ethics are basically Christian ethics, in theory at least as taught in church and school, as our own are Christian in theory. West Indians have been able to take part in a wide range of social and cultural activities in Britain. They can go to clubs and pubs with no more taboos, on their side, than those optional ones of teetotalism and non-smoking which some churches encourage.

The question of marriage is difficult. African laws of exogamy, prohibition of marriage with certain relationships (as in tables of affinity) were replaced by the slave-owners' total ban on marriage for slaves. They were regarded as the beasts, not having any affections, and in any case family bonds would have limited their movements. The old slave and evangelical literature is full of examples of this inhumanity. All of it has been abolished for over a century, of course, but it has left a nasty legacy in the low number of regular marriages, and high rate of illegitimacy. In addition, the fashion or respectability surrounding a church marriage, and the great expense involved in all its trimmings, have put legal unions beyond the reach of many people, at least till they reach affluence or enjoy a union which lasts till old age.

Many West Indians who come to this country are single, or

have an irregular or temporary union. Where they are married, and their families accompany or follow them, their love of children leads to large families. It is obviously important for the stability of society that there should not be too large a floating male population, and that families should not extend beyond economic capacity.

There are two particular elements of West Indian attitudes to marriage that distinguish them from most Asians. Firstly, there is little or no opposition to mixed marriages, with European or coloured people. There is already a great deal of racial mixture in the Caribbean. In fact, more inter-marriage, despite its strains, is one of the most useful ways of integrating a foreigner into a community, and the prejudice against colour should be weighed against the many common factors of language, religion and ethics. Secondly, West Indians normally have no objection to women going out to work, in fact this is the common practice, with great benefit to society. Women are not secluded as they are in Islam or Hinduism. The presence of West Indian women in public life in this country since the war has done much to stabilize the lives of immigrant workers.

Where there are difficulties of integration, apart from colour bias, they come from minor and often vague complaints. Black people are said to be dirty, to love overcrowding, to be noisy and violent. These are personal or social rather than racial objections. Those who are poor, living in slums, under oppressive landlords, may have difficulty in getting proper washing facilities. Such criticisms would hardly be made of those who have prospered so that they can live in the respectable suburbs where every house has a bathroom. Most people who live in the tropics are accustomed to bathing every day, if water is available. Overcrowding and Rachman-type landlords do exist, and it is a tragedy that as the old slums were being cleared new demands were made for low rents, so that new slums have arisen during the last two decades. But that is a social problem which local councils and central government alike must tackle with determination.

Noisiness belongs in part to the same problem, and is much

more noticeable where people are crowded together than in the spacious suburbs. But it is also true that West Indians are often more ebullient in nature than the repressed English, and that much of their life is lived in public owing to the nature of the tropics and openness of social organization. They delight in music; and African music, taken to America and stimulated by evangelical revivalist songs, is one of their great contributions to the modern world. It has swept over America and Europe, so that negro musicians and entertainers have broken through the stratification of American society more easily than other professions. If we do not regard this music as welcome, or highly intellectual, there is no doubt of its appeal to our younger generation, and the noise that we have to endure may be making a potent contribution to racial harmony.

It is unlikely that negro people are more violent than any others, and on their record they are probably less violent than Europeans. The civil wars, revolutions and dictatorships of modern African states, which are often mocked by those who live in slave-dictatorships in southern Africa, are not so bad as many of the devastating wars of Europe. Even in the colonial era we never ruled Africa democratically, to give an example of democracy based on universal suffrage. During twenty years in Africa I was impressed with the racial and religious tolerance of Africans generally. And there are also no apparent grounds for assertions of greater African sexuality; indeed Europeans, in South Africa as elsewhere, have left countless 'coloured' children to testify to their illegitimate sexuality. Of course, negro people, like any other, are liable to get violent if they are ground into poverty, oppressed by police, or insulted because of race or colour. But generally speaking negro people are remarkable for their good humour and long-suffering.

HINDUS

The Hindu immigrants are chiefly from India, with some from Pakistan, East Africa and the West Indies. It is only since the 'fifties that immigration from India and Pakistan has reached important numbers. Before that there was a mere trickle—of sailors who settled on land, travelling salesmen and café waiters. They were often bachelors, confined largely to dock areas, who sometimes married English women. They fitted fairly easily into social life, even to the extent of going to public houses.

Then due to rising industrial demand for workers, agents toured India, offering rosy prospects of high standards of living in England for large wages. Men came first, often settling in dormitories, and doing those unpleasant tasks, such as night duties, to which British workers objected. Many of them were skilled factory or craft workers, and some industries in this country could not have functioned without them.

Indians and Pakistanis came from lands which had much older and higher cultural traditions than the West Indies, and they were often of lighter colour, but they have had much more difficulty in fitting into British society.

Language has been a great handicap. Although English is taught in India and Pakistan, it is chiefly in higher education, and there are powerful literary languages in Hindi, Bengali, Urdu and the like. This difficulty with English was more acute for the women when they began to follow their men, and it has driven them into seclusion even more than would have been demanded by their religion or customs. Immigrant Indian men have picked up or improved their English, and children learn it in schools, but the women who stay at home may have little or no knowledge of our language, and that increases their isolation.

The position of women in Indian society has varied considerably. It is often said that there was great freedom in the olden days, before the rule of the Muslim Mughals from the sixteenth century, though this has probably been exaggerated. However the love of the human form, though rarely shown as complete nudity, appearing in countless ancient statues and paintings, contrasts with the veiling and seclusion of later times. Anthropologists like Verrier Elwin complain that modern Indian nationalists are even more Puritanical than the Muslims and Christian missionaries, in seeking to clothe and impose taboos on tribes-people who are being brought into the fold of renascent Hinduism.

In ancient India noble women were closely guarded and the law books prescribe penalties for immodesty, but Arab travellers remarked enviously that royal women often appeared without veils. All this changed under the Muslim rule of the Mughals, if not before. The system of Purdah (Parda in Urdu, from Persian *pardah*, for a veil or curtain) was introduced, whereby adult women were concealed from all men except their husbands and close relatives. Purdah was stronger in the north of India, both because it was more fully exposed to Muslim influence from Persia and because the Dravidian societies in southern India were matrilineal, and women had a good deal more freedom already than in the patrilineal Aryan societies of the north. Conversely caste restrictions were stronger in the south.

In modern times Purdah has weakened or broken down, and in immigrant communities it can hardly exist in any strength. But its influence remains in the shyness and seclusion of some Indian women from overseas. Veiling is not generally practised, though the end of the sari is useful for drawing over the face in modesty. Even Muslim women in India generally do not veil nowadays, in order to avoid making too obvious a distinction between them and Hindus, in a land where they are in a minority and might be involved in communal troubles.

Most Indians, like most ordinary people all over the world, were monogamous. But polygamy was practised in ancient times by kings and even some Brahmin priests, though one Dharma Sūtra prohibited a man taking another wife if his first had borne him sons and was of a good character. The model of marital fidelity has long been the avatar Rāma and his wife Sītā, who successfully passed through ordeals to prove her fidelity after absence from home. Since 1955 polygamy has been illegal in India for Hindus, and members of other monogamous religions like Christianity. So far Muslims are excepted from this law, but it is important for divorce cases overseas.

Traditionally, the Hindu wife serves her husband and regards him as lord or even god. She should wake him in the morning with folded hands and saying, 'Awake my Lord.' But fifty years ago Mrs Stevenson reported that many wives now say roughly, 'Come on, get up, you're late.' And we may guess how things have progressed since then.

Divorce was strictly forbidden in India in ancient times, though it is clear that it happened occasionally, and adulterous wives were very harshly treated. Husbands had fewer penalties for infidelity, but one who deserted his wife could be divorced, legal opinions giving from one to twelve years as the period after which divorce could be granted. While divorce was difficult for high castes, where marriages had been celebrated with traditional ritual, it has always been permitted among some of the lower castes according to local custom.

Sexual relationships were expounded in the Kāma Sūtra and other manuals, now translated into English. It is remarkable that this textbook was written by a priest as religious instruction, and it gives much valuable information on Indian practice. It inculcates the duty of sex life, the need for the satisfaction of both partners, the value of tenderness, and the pleasure of accompaniments of music. Although the Kāma Sūtra mentions homosexuality, it deals with it only briefly and there seems to have been less of this practice in Indian than in Greek society. Prostitution flourished, and as in ancient Greece the women were often educated *hetairae*. Others were temple dancers (*devadāsīs*, 'servants of the gods') whose occupation no doubt perpetuated ancient fertility cults. Much of this has been suppressed in modern India.

Child-marriage was notorious in India, and Mahātma Gāndhi worked hard to raise the legal age of marriage. The origins of the practice are unknown, and though it has been suggested that it was due to a desire to protect Hindu girls from Muslim overlords, it seems to have existed well before that period, though apparently it was not very common till the late Middle Ages. But fairly early the ideal ages for marriage were said to be that the husband should be three times the age of his wife, so that if he was twenty-four she would be eight. Child-marriage was not so common in the southern or eastern parts of India, and was

virtually unknown on the Malabar coast, where Christian communities were strongest. Marriages are still normally arranged
by parents, and much attention is given to horoscopes, omens
and auspicious physical marks. Light-coloured skin is also
regarded as a great advantage, a legacy of the old days of
conquest by light-skinned Aryans.

Gāndhi also worked to legalize the remarriage of virgin
widows, with some success. In medieval times widow marriage
was strictly forbidden, and Levirate marriage (a man's marrying
his brother's widow), which had earlier been allowed, came to be
prohibited. The widow was not only condemned to lifelong
celibacy but to an ascetic life, sleeping on the ground, wearing
no ornaments or perfumes, and was regarded as bringing bad
luck to any festival which she happened to witness. This sad
lot may have inclined some widows to the practice of Suttee
(satī, faithful wife), burning themselves on their husband's
funeral pyre. This was practised occasionally in ancient times,
as Greek records and the Hindu Epics show, but it seems to have
increased greatly in the Middle Ages, especially among warrior
peoples like the Rājputs. Although it is sometimes said
nowadays that the incidence of Suttee was greatly exaggerated,
and that women only willingly devoted themselves to die with
their husbands, there is contemporary evidence that force was
used to oblige some of them to conform to social expectations.
The practice of Suttee was prohibited in the British provinces
in 1829, but not till many years later in some of the princely
states.

There is considerable variation in the decorative marks (loosely
called caste marks; tilaka, 'mole', or tīkā 'spot'), made of red,
yellow or white paste, which Indian women wear. A married
woman may have a red streak in the middle parting of her hair,
as well as ornaments hanging from the parting and in her nose.
A small red spot in the middle of the forehead is a marriage
decoration, which even Christian women are adopting nowadays
since they regard it as having no religious or caste significance.
Some North Indian women have small green marks tattooed in
the middle of their brows and on their wrists, or a star tattooed

on their chin. Many women wear ear-rings, ten rings on the
fingers, ten more on the toes, bangles, anklets, girdles, head and
nose ornaments. The more specifically sectarian marks (*pundra*,
'lotus', 'line of ashes'), vertical for the followers of Vishnu and
horizontal for Shiva, worn by male ascetics, are unlikely to be
seen in Britain.

The caste system is one of the most famous, or notorious, of
Indian customs and developed to an extent unknown elsewhere.
The original four classes (which are better so called than castes),
go back to the Rig Veda, from 1500 B.C. They represent major
class and occupational divisions of Indo-European societies, but
the word used to describe them is 'colour' (*varna*), and this
probably came in time to indicate also some of the differences
between the light-skinned conquering Aryans who invaded
India at that time, and the darker though more cultured
conquered peoples. The four classes were the Brahmin priests,
warrior-rulers (Rājanya or Kshatriya), merchant farmers
(Vaishyas), and servants (Shūdras). The first three classes were
twice-born (*dvi-ja*) by initiation in adolescence; they wore white,
red and yellow threads, respectively.

The Portuguese traders introduced the word 'caste' (*casta*),
which applies more properly to the Indian groupings of 'birth'
(*jāti*). There are some three thousand of these birth castes,
stronger in the south than the north, and the product of many
forces. In addition to conquest, colour and class, factors which
are present in many lands, there has been a continual pressure of
peoples into the dead end of southern India, causing very
complex stratification. Caste distinctions were partly based on
occupations, like medieval guilds, and to this day life is affected
more deeply by being a potter, basket-maker, or silk-weaver than
by being a Vaishya or Shūdra. Trades are inherited and this
makes for rigidity of society.

Some castes were outside the class system wholly or virtually.
Some of the Shūdras were called 'excluded', according to their
professions or customs, and they were almost indistinguishable
from the Untouchables. The latter, the Outcastes who are now
called Scheduled Castes, were called Harijans, 'God's people', by

Gāndhi, and he strove to improve their religious and political status. The Outcastes performed menial or dirty tasks, especially emptying latrines and carrying corpses to cremation. They had to live outside villages and use different wells from the villagers. They might rise in status as a group, however, and there was always some fluidity in caste position. Foreigners (*mlecchas*) were also untouchable, but they too might rise in status through good conduct.

Two essential elements of caste are restrictions on marriage and food. Endogamy (marriage within the group) was insisted upon, and it appears to have existed both among the Aryan invaders and the Dravidian natives of India, as in many other parts of the world. It further complicates marriage patterns.

Commensality, or eating within the same caste, was similarly exclusive and hedged about with taboos. It was a major reason for the scruples of Brahmins, if anyone of lower caste not merely touched but even looked at or overshadowed their food. Nobody should take water or food from a lower caste, except perhaps Ganges water. For this reason Brahmins are often cooks, and water-sellers at railway stations, so that people of any caste can take from them without fear. These are ancient scruples and they die hard, and although many taboos are broken by modern travel, fears over the purity of food and drink bring continuing caste restrictions. Many Hindus will only eat food prepared by their wives, or somebody whose caste position they can trust.

Many Hindus are vegetarians, though not all. The veneration of the cow is one of the most profound beliefs and Gāndhi said it was the major element in the Hindu creed, as reverence for nature, all life, and the mother who feeds us all. Modern Puritanism has also brought prohibition of alcohol to most Indian states, and with it illicit brewing and deaths from poisoning. Most, though not all, Hindus overseas remain teetotal, and may eat meat but never beef.

The marriage and eating restrictions, in addition to any other caste taboos and the shyness and seclusion of women, help to make the Hindus overseas into closed communities. Religious differences add to their isolation, both in the variant beliefs and

rituals of one of the world's greatest religious traditions, and in
our own suspicion of 'idolatrous' ways.

SIKHS

The Sikhs are a relatively modern reform movement, arising
out of Hinduism but counted as a religion in its own right.
Gurū Nānak (1469-1533) was the founder of the Sikhs, who
were his 'disciples'. Although there were some Muslim mystical
influences in the Punjab where he lived, yet Hindu devotional
tradition (bhakti) was much more important for Nānak. The
monotheistic and non-idolatrous character of Sikh faith and
worship is Indian, and is especially interesting to Christians.
Add to this the military character of the Sikh initiates, and it
may be understood why they were particularly favoured by
British imperialism; once they had ceased to fight against it they
became some of the most loyal supporters of the Raj. During the
Second World War, while Congress leaders were in prison for
refusing co-operation with Britain, the government of the
Punjab supported us. It was rewarded for its pains by being split
down the middle in the partition of India between Hindus and
Muslims in 1948. The Sikhs rose in arms to carve out their own
kingdom, and were as vigorously opposed by the Muslims.
Eventually, after great massacres, the Sikhs were expelled from
Pakistan. Hundreds of thousands of refugees went in lorries and
bullock carts and on foot over the dusty plains into India, where
in a secular state they could practise their religion and hope for
some eventual autonomy. Fortunately their sacred city of
Amritsar was on the Indian side and it has since been restored,
along with other Indian Sikh centres.

This travail also helped to send Sikhs abroad, to East Africa
and Britain. As they are hard-working and expert technicians,
they have become valued craftsmen. Like other religious
minorities the Sikhs keep together, support one another and
look after the poor, so that few beggars are seen from their
community. This social spirit keeps them close overseas, and it is
reinforced by their particular military discipline.

It is well known that Sikhs wear turbans and beards and these are explicable as part of their history and organization. The tenth Sikh Gurū (teacher), Gobind Singh (1666-1708) had to face increasing persecution from the Muslim Mughal rulers, notably the cruel emperor Aurangzeb (1659-1707), who for fifty years harshly oppressed both Sikhs and Hindus. Gobind Singh's own father, the ninth Gurū, Tegh Bahadur, had been executed by Aurangzeb. So in 1699 Gobind Singh founded an inner group of militant Sikhs called the Khalsa, the 'pure'. These, and all their initiated descendants, swore to observe five K's. Kesh— hair and beard uncut; Kungha—steel comb in the hair; Kuccha —wearing shorts; Kara—a steel bangle on the right wrist; Kirpan—carrying a dagger. All Sikhs received into the Khalsa must also assume the name Singh ('lion'). They swear to abstain from tobacco and alcohol, not to have sexual relationships with Muslims, and not to eat meat ritually killed by Muslims (kosher). Those who have not taken the Khalsa vows, but claim to be Sikhs, are called 'slow adopters' (sahaj-dhari).

The social customs of the Sikhs, and their expulsion from Pakistan, bring them closer to some of the Hindu sects, which are of great variety, and there are some modern Sikhs who say that they will be absorbed again into the octopus-grasp of Hinduism. There are many modifications of customs in modern times. Many old men in the Punjab have venerable long beards, but young Sikhs trim or plait them, and it is said by a Sikh that 'strict adherence to the code of Gurū Gobind Singh is now more the exception than the rule.'[2] Smoking is not unusual among the upper classes, and both cigarettes and hookahs are common among Sikh peasants.

The religious beliefs of Sikhs are monotheistic, and despite the influence of Hindu bhakti they have rejected Hindu beliefs in ten or more Avatars of the deity. Yet their own ten Gurūs have virtually replaced the Hindu Avatars, as sinless mediators between God and man. The profound Hindu beliefs in Karma and reincarnation have also been retained. In social customs the

[2] K. Singh, The Sikhs, p. 179.

Sikhs have never completely freed themselves from Hindu influence. Caste distinctions were weakened in temple worship, where an outcaste might enter along with men of high caste. But inter-marriage was much more difficult, and there never has been much of this between Sikhs of different castes. Food taboos also persisted, and Sikhs of the highest caste would not eat with Untouchables or share wells with them. Many of the earliest converts to Sikhism came from the lower castes, as often happens with converts to new religions, but in time, as they prospered, they built up their own hierarchy, and imposed taboos on those who stayed below in financial and social status.

The ten Sikh Gurūs gave no teaching about the veneration of the cow that is so fundamental to Hinduism, although Gobind Singh expressed his regret at cow slaughter among Muslims. But in time the ancient cow worship returned, till Sikhs were more zealous in their protection than some Hindus. Similarly, marriage and funeral customs followed Hindu patterns, cremation was practised, the ashes carried to the Ganges where possible, and offerings were made to the ancestors. Suttee was practised by the widows of some important Sikhs. Sikh women wore the same decorative marks as Hindu women, dressed in saris and were partially veiled on occasion.

Strange though it may seem, Brahmin priests officiated in some Sikh ceremonies, as they did in Jain temples also. Horoscopes were cast at birth by learned pundits, and Brahmin priests invested Sikh rulers to the chant of Vedic hymns. They performed marriages in the Hindu pattern, and conducted funerals. All these customs show how great are the affinities of the Sikhs with Hindus, especially in social matters and the sacraments of family life. Muslim influences on Sikh thought grew less with persecution, and they have diminished even more in recent times with the expulsion of Sikhs from Pakistan and the closing of all Sikh temples there.

Sikh men remain distinctive, however, by their dress and membership of the Khalsa. They recite their own scriptures, the Ādi Granth, in the Punjabi language. They have their own temples and religious festivals. It is said that in 1966 there were thirty-five Sikh temples in Britain. At Smethwick, where there has been a notorious general election in which colour prejudice played a part, there was local protest at the supposed introduction of 'idolatry' when a Congregational church was converted into a Sikh temple. The slightest knowledge of Sikh religion would have shown that it is non-idolatrous. The Sikh religion is also missionary, in theory, but there is little evidence, either here or in East Africa, that Sikhs belong to any but Indian races, and then chiefly Punjabi. The Sikhs hold together, and as industrious communities they earn considerable respect from those who are willing to look at them fairly.

MUSLIMS

The great majority of Muslim immigrants come to Britain from Pakistan, with smaller numbers from East Africa and the West Indies. The few who come from lands like Iraq and Egypt are mostly students and not true immigrants.

Like Indians, the Pakistani immigrants were only a few sailors and waiters before 1945, and they became 'de-tribalized' more easily than when greater numbers arrived to produce some group ethos. In the 'fifties British agents toured Pakistan recruiting workers, and those who came were generally from rural or conservative backgrounds, with little knowledge of the English language or customs. Pakistani students were much better off, with more money, better command of English, and more social agencies to care for them. Now, the workers often have introductions to jobs, or friends who can help them to get work, and things are easier than with the first arrivals. However, many Pakistanis come without their families, while the wives that do come are usually illiterate and know no English, as is evident from the immigrant radio programmes put out by the BBC on Sunday mornings.

Pakistan is nearly all Muslim, with few Hindus and a handful of Christians. However, the plan to found an Islamic state has never been fully carried out, and is one cause of modern political tensions. There are a few mosques in Britain, which, on the whole, are not well attended except twice a year on the great festival days, following the Ramadān fast and during the ritual of Pilgrimage. There is an Islamic Centre in Regent's Park which serves communal purposes for intellectuals, but a long-projected mosque there has never got beyond the drawing board. A well-known mosque at Woking, Surrey, belongs to the Ahmadiyya sect, whose two main centres are in Pakistan.

As in Hinduism, it is not essential for a Muslim ever to visit a place of worship to practise his religion. Islam is essentially a layman's religion, with no ordained clergy. The ritual of five daily prayers is performed according to a simple, known pattern all over the Islamic world—at home, in the street or in the market-place. Since it involves washing, you may find your bath-room occupied by a Muslim guest, especially if he is performing several acts of prayer together.

The month of Ramadān is the ninth of the Islamic year, but as this follows the moon it gets earlier every year. In temperate regions this involves very long days in summer time. Fasting is obligatory to all healthy adult Muslims during all daylight hours of the month of Ramadān. This involves complete abstention from food and drink, though plenty may be eaten at night. In modern conditions, such as in a factory, this is very trying, and some countries, like Tunisia, make exceptions for factory workers, students, soldiers, and anyone else who feels that fasting hinders necessary work. In most countries, however, Ramadān is fully observed because it is a social custom which can be easily watched, and it is not easy to find a quiet corner for a quick drink.

Islam forbids the eating of pork, probably after an ancient Jewish practice, and in communal troubles in India the killing of pigs by Hindus and cows by Muslims has given great offence. The prohibition, of course, includes bacon and sausages. Cartridges greased with pork fat were said to be a major cause of the Indian Mutiny.

Muhammad forbade the use of wine, extended to all alcohol and most Pakistanis are teetotallers. Muslim workers not only disapprove of drinking, but want to save money by living a simple life, so as to return home as soon as possible. Gambling is also prohibited, and the puritanical Wahhābī of Arabia extend the ban even to chess, which seems excessive. A few Pakistanis gamble and like dog racing, but most of them disapprove of it.

In theory, Islamic life is governed by traditional law, sharī'ah, which applies to every activity, being based upon the Qur'ān, the Traditions, and interpreters from four major schools of law. The lawyers and teachers took the place of clergy in former times. Today there is a great deal of confusion, since much of modern life is clearly beyond the scope of canon law. Even the ban on usury, dating from the Qur'ān, is rarely taken now to apply to bank interest. Some countries, like Turkey, have abandoned Islamic law completely for a European code. Others have adopted modified forms of British, French or Swiss law, and they leave the traditional lawyers to concern themselves only with marriage, divorce and inheritance, and even these regulations are modified. Even so, most ordinary Muslims have little knowledge of the application of Islamic law. W. C. Smith,[3] whose *Islam in Modern History* is one of the most penetrating studies of the changes in Muslim life, gives an instance where a senior member of the Pakistani administration, with an Oxford degree, showed almost total ignorance of sharī'ah. 'Certainly the law of Pakistan must be the sharī'ah,' he asserted. But when pressed he said, 'The sharī'ah is the laws of the Qur'ān.' Asked if it did not include the Traditions, he stumbled. 'Well . . . anyway . . . well, that has to do with the Prophet . . . In any case, the Qur'ān is the important thing.'

The status of women is one of the most important aspects of the Muslim way of life. Veiling is not prescribed in the Qur'ān and is not practised in all Islamic countries, though some form of it exists in most of them. Most women in Pakistan still wear veils, though some of the younger ones wear very fetching nylon veils which reveal more than conceal. Women are heavily veiled from head to foot in the *burqa'* in Arabia but ninety per cent of Egyptian women are unveiled, some lands like Turkey have

[3] *Islam in Modern History*, 1957, p. 245n.

officially abolished the veil, and some independent Africans have never accepted it, for example in Somalia and Western Nigeria.

Women rarely go to mosques at the formal time of prayer, but perform their devotions at home in the same way as men, though separate from them. The Qur'ān limited the number of wives a man could take. 'If you fear that you may not act with equity in regard to the orphans, marry such of the women as seem good to you, two or three or four. But if you fear that you may not be fair, then one only . . . and give the women their dowries as a gift.' (Qur'ān: 4, 3) The context of this pronouncement of Muhammad, taken by Muslims as the very Word of God, was after the battle of Uhud. At this battle seventy-five Muslims were killed and Muhammad was concerned to make both material and financial provision for the widows and orphans of the community.

This statement has been taken as the rule of Islam, limiting the number of wives. It was easy to get round, since divorce needed only two witnesses and a formal repudiation, and it is said that the late Ibn Saud of Arabia had a hundred legal wives, but never more than four at a time.

In modern times there have been many efforts to restrict or even forbid polygamy. The Quranic text says 'if you fear that you may not be fair' to more than one wife then marry only one. Muslims argue that it is impossible to be fair to more than one wife and interpret this text as an exhortation to monogamy. Most ordinary people can only afford one partner and polygamy has been the luxury of the rich. But public opinion is against it, and it is notable that when the Shah of Persia had no male heir, and could by tradition have taken an extra wife, he preferred to divorce his wife and contract another monogamous marriage. Some modern states such as Tunisia, Turkey, Syria and Persia have forbidden polygamy or greatly restricted it. In Pakistan, men who wanted a return to Islamic ways against the infidel European style of monogamy, clamoured for the removal of Ayub Khan since his military rule had not confirmed the proposed Islamic constitution. But the women demonstrated in his favour because they preferred to have no rivals.

Most Muslims, despite *Punch* cartoons, are monogamous and their wives are often unveiled. However, cases occasionally come before our courts, in which polygamy is recognized as having been contracted in a country whose legal system permits it. The marriage of Muslims to Christians should create no barrier. The Woking Mosque publishes lists of English converts to Islam, but many of them appear to be women who have become Muslims on marrying a Muslim student or worker. This conversion is not strictly necessary. Christians are recognized in the Qur'ān as 'People of the Book'. Muhammad himself had a Christian concubine, called Mary, a political gift from the Christian ruler of Egypt, rather like President Nkrumah's Coptic wife.

Although Indian and Pakistani immigrants, in particular, have tended to live apart from the rest of society, secluded in their families or lodgings, and cut off by language and custom, there are signs of change. There is evidence that they are realizing that their problems demand some participation in local and national affairs. One sign of this has been the appearance of Pakistani candidates in municipal elections, but even more surprising is the fact that those Pakistanis who voted did not choose their own racial candidate, but five out of six voted for the Labour Party candidate. This is one of the more hopeful signs of the acceptance by immigrants of participation in the life of the society around them, and it is important that British society should respond and help this integration in every possible way.

Dr E. G. Parrinder is Reader in the Study of Comparative Religions, at King's College, University of London.

The Problems and Methods of Teaching the Comparative Study of Religion in Schools

F. H. HILLIARD

THE PROBLEMS

Is it justified?

There are still some teachers who would ask this question. They take the view, and rightly in my opinion, that the main function of religious education in British schools is to awaken interest in Christianity: to develop knowledge about and insight into the nature and significance of the Christian faith. I say Christianity because the whole range of formal education, although it may have a wider view, tends to concentrate upon various aspects of the traditions and culture in which the pupils are growing up. Thus in the schools of Great Britain it is not customary to teach in relation to the study of literature or languages a wide range of both which covers not only Europe but the Middle and Far East as well. We do not offer our pupils a choice between, say, English, French, German, Scandinavian and Islamic literatures, Chinese, Sanskrit and so on. We put the main emphasis upon English language and literature and offer additionally the possibility of studying the language and literature of some country with which Great Britain has close links, French, German, Spanish and more recently, on a small scale, Russian. So also with history and geography, though to a lesser degree, because of the nature of the subject.

This clearly is an important practical consideration which must be borne in mind most carefully whenever we consider the place which should be given to the study of religions other than Christianity (or to some extent Judaism) in the schools of

Great Britain. People sometimes talk without careful consideration of all that is involved as though the great advantage to be
gained from introducing the study of religions other than
Christianity or Judaism into the classrooms of schools in this
country would be that it would enable the pupils to choose for
themselves which religion they preferred at some stage during
adolescence. This, of course, is complete nonsense. Not only does
it offend against a cardinal principle of educational procedures, as
previously indicated; it is also completely unrealistic in practice.
One has only to ask oneself the question how many youngsters,
at the end of a secondary school course, would be in a position
or in fact would be likely to want to become Muslims, Buddhists,
Hindus or what you will, to see that this point of view is
utterly unrealistic.

No, if the teaching of the non-Christian religions is to be
justified in the context of the curricula of schools in Great
Britain then it has to be justified on much more impressive and
realistic grounds than these. How then is it to be justified?

(a) First of all, it is justifiable because as a matter of fact
Christianity is but one among the various religions of the world,
and what is more, one among several equally great religions,
judged in terms of both the numbers of people who are attracted
to them and the general extent of their influence. Christians
have, of course, been aware of this fact for centuries but never so
conscious of it as they are in our century because faster means
of communication have brought the various parts of the world
more closely together. The increasing rapidity of modern communications makes ours a constantly shrinking world. How
much it goes on shrinking in this sense we are reminded when
we are told that Concorde, the new supersonic airliner, is going
to cut by half the duration of journeys to various parts of the
world. Every time astronauts are blasted off from Russia or Cape
Kennedy one realizes just how small our world has become,
when it is possible for its inhabitants to make their way from
here into outer space in the matter of a few days.

(b) Any teaching about religion which goes on in schools
can therefore no longer allow itself to be confined to the study

of that religion which predominates in a particular area of the world. Every time our children look at television programmes, listen to the radio or open newspapers they are reminded by what they see and hear that there are men and women in other parts of the world whose dress, behaviour, customs and in some cases attitudes to life are fundamentally different from those of the people they meet around them every day. Futhermore, they discover that a good many of these people have grown up in an environment which has been influenced by religious beliefs which have themselves accounted for many of these striking differences.

(c)   This brings me to the third reason which justifies the teaching in schools of what may be called world religions. It is the children's interest in the subject. There is considerable evidence to show that they are fascinated by those very differences previously outlined. The fact that Hindus or Sikhs in India, Buddhists in Ceylon or Muslims in Africa and the Middle East dress differently, worship in different sorts of buildings from the ones they are used to, have different religious customs and beliefs—all this fascinates young people and they are eager to discover more about it. This alone would be sufficient to justify this kind of teaching. At a time when we are constantly being reminded that adolescents in particular are put off rather than attracted to religious education it is surely extremely important that one should try to satisfy what curiosity and interest they do have about certain aspects of religion.

(d)   But in addition to these reasons, there are others. During the last twenty years or so there have been signs of a growing desire on the part of Christians in various parts of the world to enter into what is fashionably called 'a dialogue' with people of other religious beliefs and persuasions. This represents a significant change of attitude as compared with the period before the Second World War when it would be true to say that there were comparatively few within the Christian churches who had advanced beyond the notion that one should take account of the adherents of religions other than Christianity only with a view to converting them. Also, up to that time the number of those who were concerned to study the non-Christian religions from a standpoint which did not imply the superior status of Christianity were very few indeed. Since the end of the Second World War some interesting and refreshing changes have come over both these attitudes and there are many thoughtful Christians today who see that they must abandon the remains of the old attitudes to the adherents of non-Christian religions and approach them and their faiths in attitudes of humility and out of a desire to discover what it is in them which has attracted and attracts.

In answer to the question, 'Is the teaching of CSR justified?' I would say quite categorically that if as a result of a course in religious education in a school in Great Britain pupils are not given some opportunity of discovering something about other men's religions, they will probably have, and justifiably, some reason for thinking that they have been kept in the dark about an aspect of religion which is so important that they certainly ought to have been given the chance of discovering more about it.

Time Allocation

The next problem that confronts a teacher who wants to do something about introducing this kind of teaching into his syllabus is how to find time for it without sacrificing other parts which seem to him to be important. It is essential that one bears in mind the fact that it is by no means always customary for RE to receive two full periods a week in the time-table. Indeed in far too many schools the customary allocation is one period a week. In schools where this situation prevails the teacher is obviously faced with a real dilemma. With this time allocation it is difficult enough to do justice to the main function of RE in relation to Christianity. If he is to give at least a reasonable allocation of time to short courses dealing with other religions then something important has to be sacrificed. There are however many teachers who would feel that even in this difficult situation room has still to be found, for the reasons already stated, for the inclusion of at least short courses dealing with world religions. If one is faced with difficult choices of this kind, then in the last resort they merely underline the necessity that the teacher should develop the habit of making a most careful distribution of time overall in relation to the main subjects which he thinks need to be covered, and that he train himself and his pupils to make the most effective use of the limited time which is available.

At what age level(s)?

Next there is the problem: At what level or levels in formal education should teaching about world religions be introduced into the curriculum? Here one must recognize that there are two schools of thought. On the one hand some teachers argue that it is important that children should learn as soon as possible, first about the fact of the existence of religions other than their own, and second to treat them with respect. They argue therefore that juniors should begin to become acquainted with one or two of the facts about world religions, and that they should be introduced to them in such a way as encourages them even in these early years to regard them and the people who believe in them with the same sort of respect which they give to their own religion. There have been some interesting attempts made in this direction.

Most teachers who are sympathetic to this whole subject would agree that all the younger school leavers, (that is, those who leave school as soon as possible after they reach the statutory leaving age, and those who leave grammar or comprehensive schools at the age of sixteen without entering a sixth form) should have included in the last one or two years of their RE course in school some teaching about world religions.

Certainly most would strongly agree that room should be made in the one or two years' course which sixth-formers take for a somewhat deeper study of certain aspects of the whole subject.

How can the Christian (Jewish) teacher do justice to religions which he/she knows only from the outside?

This problem is in many ways the most acute of all. Most thoughtful and experienced RE teachers would probably agree that religious education is concerned with more than what used to be called religious knowledge. That is to say, religious education, though it must still be concerned to a considerable extent with introducing children to certain factual knowledge about their own religion, has a larger and more difficult task to achieve. It has to awaken in pupils interest in what religion is and what it offers to people in their whole attitude to human life in general and their own life in particular. It has also to help them to develop 'a way of knowing', or a kind of insight which enables them to see what kind of thing religion is, as distinct say from science or the arts. In other words, religious education is not merely concerned to teach 'that', but also to teach 'how'. It has to enable pupils to 'get inside' religion so that they can see what it is all about. Moreover, it must try to do all this in as objective a way as possible so that there is no suggestion that religious education is concerned with 'converting' children to religion. Its purpose is to open doors of experience to them rather than to encourage them to pass through.

Most teachers would agree that this is a difficult enough task even when one starts from the assumption that teacher and pupils at least share in a common culture and tradition in which one main religious tradition has played an influential part. In this country the teaching of religion in schools can be more meaningfully related to the Christian tradition because, even if to a lesser extent than at other times in this century, the practice of Christianity and the influence of Christian beliefs and attitudes still form some part of our way of life. There is therefore a good deal of common ground between teacher and pupil here which can be taken for granted. How different the situation is when the same teacher is trying to do the same sort of job in relation to other religious traditions which have not formed part of the main stream of religious life in this country, and which he and his pupils can therefore know only at second hand. In what sense can teaching children about these other religions be described as religious education in the same sense in which the term is used of the teaching of Christianity in the main part of the RE course? One must face the fact that there are bound to be significant differences, see clearly what they are and accept the limitations involved. So far as any RE course is concerned, it is not a problem to communicate to pupils certain factual information about religion. The vast amount of literature which is now available in English publications about the main religious traditions of the world provides teachers with ample material from which to ensure that pupils learn accurately some of the facts about world religions. At this point a comment needs to be made: it is quite impossible for a teacher to begin to do justice to this kind of teaching unless he or she resorts to some of the more dependable and valuable works which have been written about the separate religions. If one's reading starts from one of the books which survey briefly world religions in general, this can be no more than an aperitif. The meal, meta-phorically speaking, must proceed to a choice of the vintage wines which are on the menu, in other words, resort must then be made to at least some of the sizeable volumes dealing with different aspects of the various religions before one really attempts to put together that part of a course for use in school.

But to come back to the main question. It may also be the case that teachers who have been brought up against a background of Christian belief and practice can enter at greater depth into the attitudes, aspirations, feelings and beliefs of the adherents of what may be called the great 'Semitic' religions, that is, Judaism and Islam. Christianity had its origins within the framework of Judaism, so also did Islam. The language, the literature, the basic ideas of God and man, of sin, of judgment, of the after-life and so on, all have a good deal in common so far as these great religions are concerned. It is therefore possible for a Christian teacher to go a good deal further in sympathy, insight and appreciation where his teaching of these religions is concerned. Moreover, it is perfectly possible for teachers, and sometimes their pupils, to visit a local synagogue and to talk with members of the community who worship in it. In certain parts of the country it is now easier than it used to be to do the same thing in connection with a mosque and a Muslim community.

But all this must not blind us to the difficulty which any teacher will certainly experience when it comes to dealing with the great religions which dominate life in the Far East such as Hinduism and Buddhism. Here attitudes to the Divine, the nature of human existence, the nature of evil and suffering and so on are so fundamentally different from those which emerge from the teaching of the Semitic religions that it is extremely difficult for most teachers to be sure that they have the insight to do justice to the religion concerned.

THE METHODS

Juniors

Some teachers think it important that children of junior school age should begin to become aware of the existence of religions other than their own. At this stage children are generally capable of thinking in concrete, though not in abstract terms. It follows that they can best be introduced to world religions by learning about the lives of the founders and other leading figures connected with them, about the buildings used for worship and the activities which take place in them.

Not all religions are traditionally associated with a founder-figure, but enough historical or semi-historical tradition exists for an outline of the life and work of Muhammad, Zoroaster, Gautama, Confucius and Lao-Tzu.

Visits can usually be arranged to a synagogue, and nowadays sometimes to a mosque. Pictures, including film-strips and films, are available on temples, shrines and religious ceremonial in India and Japan, as well as those connected with the other religions mentioned above. Nor should it be forgotten that children of this age may be in daily contact in their schools with immigrant children whose religious background is Hindu, Sikh or Islamic.

The aim at this stage will be simple and uncomplicated—to

encourage awareness of the existence of other religions, to arouse interest and to lay the foundations of respect for other men's religions.

Younger School-Leavers

If justice is to be done to the study of Christianity there will be little time in the secondary school to devote to world religions before the fourth year. The syllabus in this year ought however to include work on the great living religions, not only because at this stage pupils are ready for it, but also because for many of them this will be their last year at school. If it is accepted that no pupil should come to the end of his religious education course without some knowledge of religions other than his own, then a course, even a short one, on world religions is a 'must' for the younger school-leaver.

Two practical considerations must be borne in mind in planning such a course. The school leaver of 15 years will often be of 'average or less than average ability'. He will be more interested in the 'real' world of people and their activities rather than in a study of their ideas and ideals. The kind of course which is likely to arouse his interest will therefore be an extension of the work mentioned above for junior-aged children. It can, of course, be somewhat more detailed and of wider compass than that provided in the junior school.

The actual organization of the course will depend upon the way in which the whole of the work of the school is planned at this stage. It is becoming increasingly common for secondary schools to devise integrated courses in the Humanities for the young school-leaver in which religious education has a place. It is obvious that close and valuable integration with geographical and historical material is possible in the case of work on world religions of the sort here envisaged. Indeed, it can be done effectively only with the close support of geographical and historical material, so that integration is here a distinct advantage. Where religious education remains separately time-tabled, the supporting background material has to be provided within a more restricted allocation of time.

Here, too, the aim of such a course will be straightforward and unambitious: to arouse interest in some of the basic facts about the great religions and, in the course of so doing, to encourage sympathy and respect for other men's faiths. This in itself can be an important contribution to international as well as religious understanding.

Sixth Formers

It is not possible to generalize about 'sixth formers'. As more pupils stay on at school after the age of 16, so sixth forms tend to be made up of some pupils who hope to proceed to a university or college of education, and others who intend to acquire further 'O' level or even CSE qualifications before entering employment or professional training. Sixth forms may thus be made up of pupils whose intellectual abilities vary considerably and this fact will have a close bearing on the type of work which is possible in connection with the study of world religions.

In general, courses for pupils at this stage can attempt to deal with some of the important religious ideas and ideals which are embedded in the main religious traditions. They will thus be breaking fresh ground as compared with the courses lower down the secondary school. More able pupils will be capable of appreciating the differences between ideas of the divine in Hinduism and Buddhism on the one hand, and the 'Semitic' religions of Judaism, Christianity and Islam on the other. Similarly, differences in attitudes to the nature of man, of evil, suffering and the nature of the 'good life'; in the nature of sacred scriptures, about worship, its character and purpose, will be able to be examined.

Less able pupils will still find it more congenial to approach some of these topics by a closer study of the practices of the great religions rather than the beliefs as such, and will probably need to work at less depth than the potential undergraduates in the sixth form. It follows therefore that parallel rather than single-type courses need to be planned.

Some teachers may prefer to concentrate upon a study in depth of two religions rather than attempt to cover all the main living religions. A study of the ideals about God or worship in say Islam and Judaism, or of 'the good life' in the Bhagavad Gita of Hinduism and in the Lotus scripture of Buddhism can be very rewarding to more able pupils, even if more demanding.

It will be obvious that effective teaching about world religions at this level demands of the teacher the kind of knowledge and insights which can be acquired only by reading and study in some depth. A wide variety of scholarly and dependable books in English exists and so makes such study possible. Time and effort are the price which the teacher must be willing to pay if his teaching is to gain the respect of his pupils and to achieve the ends which are possible through work at this level.

Professor F. H. Hilliard is Professor of Education, University of Birmingham.

The Comparative Study of Religion in Colleges of Education

ERIC J. SHARPE

Interest in the comparative study of religion in various types of educational institution is now recognized to be very widespread indeed. A few years ago it was practically confined to universities and a small number of theological colleges, but at the present time the subject is in process of recognition throughout our educational system. It will be obvious that a key role in this process is played by the colleges of education, since they train virtually all teachers at the primary level and many at the secondary level (or their equivalents within the comprehensive system).

However, the detailed features of this development have not as yet been documented. Its general features are well enough known, but little has been done to investigate the actual attitudes to CSR currently held at various academic levels. The main questions which need to be asked are:

(a) to what extent CSR is in fact being incorporated into the teaching syllabuses of, in this case, colleges of education;

(b) what is the attitude to CSR of those at present engaged in RE teaching in such colleges; and

(c) what practical and administrative problems affect the provision of CSR instruction for future teachers?

With this in mind, a brief questionnaire was sent to a number of colleges of education in the London area, Cheshire, Derbyshire and Lancashire. It was hoped by this means to obtain something of a cross-section of opinion. It goes without saying that this survey does not claim to represent the country as a whole. Nor does it offer statistics. Given more time, a useful full-scale survey might be made, from which an overall picture could be derived.

Twenty-four colleges sent replies, usually provided by the Principal, or by the head of the RE or Divinity department.[1] Some of these were very full indeed, and I only regret that space does not permit me to incorporate longer quotations into the text of this report.

A number of these colleges were church-related (Roman Catholic, Anglican or Methodist), but this did not seem to make any appreciable difference to their attitude to CSR, which was almost without exception strikingly positive. In fact this was the most outstanding feature of the enquiry; perhaps little proof of this was needed, but here was ample confirmation.

However, not all the colleges approached are currently providing separate courses in CSR. A number stated that they did not give formal teaching in the subject, but went on to qualify this by saying that they do their best to relate RE teaching to the world situation. What this means in practice is that although formal CSR courses may not be given, information about religions other than Christianity, and suitable comparative material, are provided wherever possible. One college reported, for instance, that they had no intention of setting up CSR courses 'as a separate academic discipline', but advocated its integration into RE studies. Main subject RE and B.Ed. students are normally given the opportunity to orientate themselves in at least the basic teachings of world religions; in curriculum studies this is naturally a variable. One college noted that 'Individual students frequently choose a topic in the area of comparative religion as their main field, special study topic.'

Some firmly negative attitudes were expressed. For instance:

On the whole I am not in favour of such courses because: they tend to cover too wide a field and become superficial; I have doubts about the ability to transmit accurately a faith which is much removed from the lecturer's sympathies; students find it even more

---

[1] I should like at this point to express my thanks to those who wrote the answers.

difficult to "get inside" one other religion, much less several; I would be in favour of the principle that such courses open up alternative views to students, but I think this can best be done in other ways.

And a lecturer wrote that instead of courses in CSR, 'I would prefer to engage in dialogue with a member of another religion— it is difficult to visualize convincing teaching from outside a faith. A dialogue brings faiths together.' A different approach was taken by one respondent who stressed that not all students have identical needs or are going to find themselves in identical situations:

I do not consider that Comparative Religion *ought* to form part of the teacher training course for all students. It is desirable that some should have a knowledge of the subject and this is one of the reasons why our subsidiary course was introduced. With an increasing immigrant population knowledge is a prerequisite of tolerance and we have in mind teachers entering schools with a population of mixed faiths.

But most lecturers were quite firm in their insistence that the demands of the present day must be met, and that these include some knowledge of non-Western religious and cultural traditions. The most common 'local' reason was, as was only to be expected, the presence in this country of increasingly large immigrant communities. So, to take only one of a number of examples, one college stated that '. . . a purely Bible-based approach to RE is inadequate to equip teachers to meet questions from immigrant children of non-Christian parents.'

This was, however, neither the only nor the most important reason given for advocating more CSR. Some very searching questions are evidently being asked about the traditional priority of Christianity in college RE teaching. Here are some outstanding opinions, reflecting both the new situation of Christianity in the world and the new world perspective:

Religion is inadequately studied except in the context of world religion (e.g. distinctive elements in Christianity can only be seen and evaluated when other religions have been studied.

And,

Christian isolationalism is no longer, if it ever was, a practical possibility. Though local factors have their role, the teacher of tomorrow teaches in a world situation. The respectability of the Christian position and claim demands that the setting of its study be comparative.

Another reply said that '. . . some understanding of other countries and their cultures is now an essential part of a reasonable education . . .' And again,

In the "global village" of today's world, the future teacher of religious education in schools cannot afford to indulge in Christian parochialism; this situation is most obviously brought home to us in this country by the immigrant problem, which many of our students will encounter in years to come. In general, if religious studies are to be fully "open" and descriptive, they must range over the widest possible spectrum.

These two motives—Christian perspective and immigrant teaching—were combined by the Principal of a Roman Catholic college:

Comparative religion ought to form part of the course because of the cultural value for the students and especially because it should help them to appreciate their own faith. With the growing numbers of people of other faiths in this country it has become necessary for future teachers to know something of the beliefs of these children when they meet them in school.

And on a slightly different academic level, the head of an RE department wrote that:

Our religious studies course has a strong bent to philosophy of religion, with some psychology of religion; it would be a serious defect not to relate this to other than familiar religions. It also stimulates a good learning situation . . .

Most answers to the questionnaire noted that there is a great gulf fixed between the ideal and the actual in CSR. So while many lecturers would like nothing better than to extend their work in this area, there are a variety of practical reasons why this is not possible. Some were doubtful about the students' capacity for absorbing the material, feeling that it is hard enough to teach elements of the Christian tradition, without launching out into strange waters. For example, a college lecturer, who felt that

. . . there is no fundamental objection to teaching comparative religion, indeed it should be encouraged—but one has to bear in mind that the time allowable for the study of an academic subject in a college of education is not as great as within a university (and it is very broken time), and further not all colleges of education divinity students have a profundity of either theology (of their own) or philosophy—a fairly fundamental basis for any successful divinity student, and indeed possibly very necessary where a study of comparative religion is concerned!

Other practical objections voiced by more than one lecturer included, as one put it, '. . . the lack of specialists in this field to provide teaching of a standard comparable with that of other areas of theology.' These sentiments were echoed by the lecturer who lamented the shortage of '. . . specialist lecturers who know enough about it [CSR] to make the study meaningful, and not just "pulp-press" stuff.' There can be no doubt that the shortage of suitably qualified staff is felt deeply in a number of quarters. This involves the question of what exactly constitutes a 'qualified' lecturer—a question to which there is no simple answer. It must be recognized that in many cases a genuine interest, and some intelligent reading of reliable literature, may be of more value than a formal university course. But many lecturers lack the time and inclination to pursue such a course of study on their own; they tend to look upon the field as too vast and amorphous to justify their amateur efforts. Occasionally one felt that the subject is being 'dealt with' in some colleges by unsuitable staff; but it would be wise not to be too categorical on this point. There is evidently ample room for the assistance which can be provided by university departments of CSR in setting up courses for those lecturers and teachers who would like to do more in this field, but are hampered by lack of knowledge.

A cognate difficulty was felt to be the lack of suitable literature. A lecturer wrote:

The biggest problem in the training of teachers is the lack of material which would help a teacher of pupils from other faiths. The standard books on world religion may give the origin, the theology and the major religious observances, but they don't give any help in warning the teacher about the numerous ways in which he or she might unintentionally offend against the customs or practices of another community . . . The production of this kind of material is an urgent necessity.

Finally, there was the timetable problem, and the problem of modifying the existing syllabuses in order to make room for more CSR. A college lecturer wrote rather plaintively: 'If I wish to alter the syllabus, the cumbersome machinery of the Institute of Education means that such a step will take nearly three years,' and recorded that she would prefer 'more comparative religion and less church history'. To end on an optimistic note, this was the judgment expressed by the Principal of a college:

Change comes but slowly. To include more comparative study—which I consider desirable—demands the exclusion of traditionally important Christian material and the employment of relevantly qualified staff. Both of which pose problems. But problems exist to be overcome!

Dr Eric J. Sharpe is Lecturer in Comparative Religion, University of Manchester.

On-going Work

At the conference held at Shap in 1969 a Working Party was established to consider the role of comparative religion in education. It is composed of three university teachers in comparative religion, seven lecturers in education, and nine teachers. The suggested aims of the Working Party are:

(1) To identify the practical problems at various educational levels involved in teaching about world religions.
(2) To study and provide relevant syllabus material.
(3) To generate new ideas, to explore the possibilities of future conferences and in-service training courses for teachers.
(4) To act as a clearing house for information on visual aids, books, conferences or working parties on related topics.

Further details can be obtained from the secretary, John R. Hinnells, who can be contacted via Oriel Press Ltd., 27, Ridley Place, Newcastle upon Tyne NE1 8LH.

Bibliography

RELIGIOUS EDUCATION

Alves, Colin, *Religion and the Secondary School*, S.C.M., London, 1968.
Blackham, H. J., *Religion in a Modern Society*, Constable, London, 1966 (Chapter 5, 'Religion in Schools').
British Humanist Association, *Religious Instruction and Education*, British Humanist Association, 1969. A report by National Opinion Polls Ltd., obtainable from B.H.A., 13, Prince of Wales Terrace, London, W.8., Price 5s.
Cousin, B., *Introducing Children to World Religions*, The Council of Christians and Jews, One Shilling Series.
Cox, E., *Changing Aims in Religious Education*, Routledge and Kegan Paul, London, 1966.
Goldman, R. J., *Religious Thinking from Childhood to Adolescence*, Routledge and Kegan Paul, London, 1964.
Hilliard, F. H., *The Teacher and Religion*, James Clarke, London, 1963.
—, *Teaching Children About World Religions*, Harrap, London, 1961.
Loukes, H., *Teenage Religion*, S.C.M., London, 1961.
—, *New Ground in Christian Education*, S.C.M., London, 1965.
Macbeath, A., *Experiments in Living* (Gifford Lectures, 1948/9), Macmillan, London, 1952. (On the relations between morality and religion.)
Macy, C. J. (Ed.), *Let's Teach Them Right* (18 papers exemplifying current thinking on religious and moral education), Pemberton Books, London, 1969.
Mathews, H. F., *Revolution in Religious Education*, Religious Education Press, London, 1966.

May, P. R. and Johnston, O. R., *Religion in Our Schools*. Hodder and Stoughton, London, 1968.

Smart, N., *Secular Education and the Logic of Religion*, Routledge and Kegan Paul, London, 1968.

Wedderspoon, A. G., *Religious Education 1944-1984*, Allen and Unwin, London, 1966.

Wilson, J. (Ed.), *An Introduction to Moral Education*, Pelican, London, 1968.

COMPARATIVE STUDY OF RELIGION

(Reference should also be made to the footnotes in Dr Sharpe's article, pp. 1-19).

GENERAL BOOKS

Anderson, J. N. (Ed.), *The World's Religions*, Inter-Varsity Fellowship, London, 1950.

Brandon, S. G. F., *Man and His Destiny in the Great Religions*, Manchester University Press, Manchester, 1962.

Brow, R., *Religion—Origins and Ideas*, Tynedale Press, London, 1966.

Eliade, M., *From Primitive to Zen*, a Thematic Sourcebook on the History of Religions, Collins, London, 1967.

—, *Myth and Reality*, Allen and Unwin, London, 1963.

—, *Patterns in Comparative Religion*, Sheed and Ward, London, 1958.

Finegan, J., *The Archaeology of World Religions*, Princeton, 1952.

Gennep, A. van, *The Rites of Passage*, Routledge and Kegan Paul, London, 1965.

Happold, F. C., *Mysticism a Study and an Anthology*, Pelican, London, 1964.

Hilliard, F. H., *How Men Worship*, Routledge and Kegan Paul, London, 1965.

History of Religions, International Association for the, *The Impact of Modern Culture on Traditional Religions*, Proceedings of the XIth International Congress of the International Association for the History of Religions, Brill, Leiden, 1968. .

James, E. O., *Comparative Religion*, University Paperbacks, Methuen, 1961.

—, *History of Religions*, Teach Yourself Series, Hodder and Stoughton, London, 1964.

Ling, T., *A History of Religions East and West*, Macmillan, London, 1968.

Noss, J. B., *Man's Religions*, Macmillan, New York, reprinted 1968.

Parrinder, E. G., *Worship in the World's Religions*, Faber and Faber, London, 1961.

—, *A Book of World Religions*, Hulton Educational Publications, London, 1965. (Suitable for use in the classroom.)

Pritchard, E. Evans, *Theories of Primitive Religion*, Clarendon, Oxford, 1965.

Ringgren, H. and Ström, A. V., *Religions of Mankind, Yesterday and Today*, Oliver and Boyd, Edinburgh, 1967.

Smart, N., *World Religions: A Dialogue*, Pelican, London, 1966.

Spencer, S., *Mysticism in World Religion*, Pelican, London, 1963.

Zaehner, R. C. (Ed.), *The Concise Encyclopaedia of Living Faiths*, Hutchinson, London, 1959.

—, *Mysticism Sacred and Profane*, Oxford Paperbacks, London, 1961.

INDIA

Basham, A. L., *The Wonder that was India*, Sidgwick and Jackson, London, 1954.

Conze, E., *Buddhism, Its Essence and Development*, Faber and Faber, London, 1951.

—, *Buddhist Scriptures*, Penguin Classics, London, reprinted 1960.

—, *Buddhist Thought in India*, Allen and Unwin, London, 1962.

Dasgupta, S., *A History of Indian Philosophy*, 5 vols., Cambridge University Press, London, 1951-5.

—, *Indian Idealism*, Cambridge University Press, London, 1962.

de Bary, Wm. Theodore (Ed.), *Sources of Indian Tradition*, in the series Introduction to Oriental Civilizations, Oxford University Press, London, 1960.

Eliot, C., *Hinduism and Buddhism*, 3 vols., Routledge and Kegan Paul, London, 1921.

Elwin, V., *The Tribal World of Verrier Elwin*, Oxford University Press, 1964.

Gonda, J., *Die Religionen Indiens*, 2 vols., Stuttgart, 1960. (One of the best recent scholarly books, for those able to read German.)

Hutton, J. H., *Caste in India*, Oxford University Press, 1946.

Ions, V., *Indian Mythology*, Hamlyn, London, 1968 (amply illustrated).

Ling, T., *Buddha, Marx and God*, Macmillan, London, 1966.

Radhakrishnan, S., *Indian Philosophy*, 2 vols., Allen and Unwin, London, 1951.

Renou, L. (Ed.), *Hinduism*, Washington Square Press, New York, reprinted 1967.

Thomas, P., *Hindu Religion, Customs and Manners*, Taraporevala, Bombay, 3rd ed. 1956.

—, *The Life of Buddha*, Routledge and Kegan Paul, London, 3rd ed., 1949.

Zaehner, R. C., *Hindu Scriptures*, Everyman Library, Dent, London, 1966.

—, *Hinduism*, Oxford University Press, London, 1967.

—, *The Bhagavad-Gita*, Oxford University Press, London, 1969.

THE SIKHS

Archer, J. C., *The Sikhs*, Princeton, 1946.

Mcleod, W. H., *Gurū Nanak and the Sikh Religion*, Oxford University Press, London, 1968.

Singh, K., *The Sikhs*, Allen and Unwin, London, 1953.

ISLAM

Arberry, A. J., *The Koran Interpreted*, London, 1955. (Probably the best translation of the Koran available.)

Guillaume, A., *Islam*, Pelican, London, 1962.

Hitti, P. K., *History of the Arabs*, Macmillan, London, 1946.

Iqbal, M., *The Reconstruction of Religious Thought in Islam*, Luzac, London, 2nd ed. 1958.

Levy, R., *The Social Structure of Islam*, Cambridge University Press, London, 1957.

Lewis, B., *The Arabs in History*, Grey Arrow, London, 1958.

Rahman, F., *Islam*, Weidenfeld and Nicolson, London, 1967.

Smith, W. C., *Islam in Modern History*, Mentor, 1963.

—, *Modern Islam in India*, London, 1947.

Tritton, A. S., *Islam*, Hutchinson University Library, London, 1966.

Watt, W. Montgomery, *Muhammed Prophet and Statesman*, Oxford University Press, London, 1961.

AFRICA

Lienhardt, G., *Divinity and Experience*, the Religion of the Dinka, Clarendon, Oxford reprinted 1967.

Middleton, J., *The Lugbara of Uganda*, Holt, Rinehart and Winston, New York, 1961.

Parrinder, E. G., *African Traditional Religion*, S.P.C.K., London, 1962.

—, *African Mythology*, Hamlyn, London, 1967 (amply illustrated).

—, *Religion in Africa*, Penguin, London, 1969.

Pritchard, E. Evans, *Nuer Religion*, Clarendon, Oxford, 1967.

Smith, E. W. (Ed.), *African Ideas of God*, Edinburgh House Press, London, 1950.

THE WEST INDIES

(Further to Dr Parrinder's article, pp. 73-7.)

Caldecott, A., *The Church in the West Indies*, SPCK, London, 1898.

Macmillan, W. M., *Warning from the West Indies*, Penguin, London, 1938.

Mathieson, W. L., *British Slavery and its Abolition*, Longmans, London, 1926.

Parry, J. H., *A Short History of the West Indies*, Macmillan, London, 1963.

BOOKS FOR THE YOUNGER CHILDREN

Oxfam Books, 274, Banbury Road, Oxford, supply a number of illustrated books produced in India for young children, some of them containing Indian folk tales, e.g., *Nagmati* (price 3s. 6d.) and books on Indian children at work and play, e.g., M. Norris, *Young India*, 1966. There is also a series of four on the World's Villages, edited by T. O. Newnham (Longmans, 1967, price 3s. 9d. each) for use at secondary level.

Others of interest include:

Clayton, R., *South Asia*, Weidenfeld and Nicolson, London 1967.

Hatch, J., *Africa—The Rebirth of Self Rule*, Oxford University Press, London, 1967.

Zinkin, T., *India and Her Neighbours*, Oxford Children's Reference Library, Oxford University Press, London, 1967.

(For up-to-date lists contact the Education Department of Oxfam.)

Note: Borough Road College acts as an information centre and a clearing-house for the reception and distribution of information relevant to the teaching of world religions. Lists, which include a calendar of major festivals (September to August), a selected bibliography and sources of audio-visual aids can be obtained by sending a postal order for 3s. and a stamped and addressed foolscap envelope to The Head of the Divinity Department, (DW), Borough Road College, Isleworth, Middlesex, England.

Notes

NOTES

NOTES